Textbook Outlines, Highlights, and Practice Quizzes

Essential Foundations of Economics

by Robin Bade, 7th Edition

All "Just the Facts101" Material Written or Prepared by Cram101 Textbook Reviews

Title Page

"Just the Facts101" is a Content Technologies publication and tool designed to give you all the facts from your textbooks. Register for the full practice test for each of your chapters for virtually any of your textbooks.

Facts101 has built custom study tools specific to your textbook. We provide all of the factual testable information and unlike traditional study guides, we will never send you back to your textbook for more information.

YOU WILL NEVER HAVE TO HIGHLIGHT A BOOK AGAIN!

Facts101 StudyGuides

All of the information in this StudyGuide is written specifically for your textbook. We include the key terms, places, people, and concepts... the information you can expect on your next exam!

Facts101

Only Facts101 gives you the outlines, highlights, and PRACTICE TESTS specific to your textbook. Facts101 sister Cram101.com is an online application where you'll discover study tools designed to make the most of your limited study time.

www.Cram101.com

Copyright © 2016 by Content Technologies, Inc. All rights reserved.

"FACTS101"®, "Cram101"® and "Never Highlight a Book Again!"® are registered trademarks of Content Technologies, Inc.

ISBN(s): 9781538837375. PUBE-4.20161228

STUDYING MADE EASY

This Cram101 notebook is designed to make studying easier and increase your comprehension of the textbook material. Instead of starting with a blank notebook and trying to write down everything discussed in class lectures, you can use this Cram101 textbook notebook and annotate your notes along with the lecture.

Our goal is to give you the best tools for success.

For a supreme understanding of the course, pair your notebook with our online tools at www.cram101.com

Our Online Access program is a simple way for us to keep our promise and provide you the best studying tools, regardless of where you purchased your Cram101 textbook notebook. As long as you let us know you are intereested in a free online access account we will set it up for you for 180 days.

Online Access:

SIMPLE STEPS TO GET A FREE ACCOUNT:
Email Travis.Reese@cram101.com
Include:
Order number
ISBN of Guide
Retailer where purchased

facts101

Essential Foundations of Economics
Robin Bade, 7th

CONTENTS

1. Getting Started, ... 5
2. The U.S. and Global Economies, ... 17
3. The Economic Problem, ... 33
4. Demand and Supply, ... 41
5. Elasticities of Demand and Supply, ... 50
6. Efficiency and Fairness of Markets, ... 60
7. Government Actions in Markets, ... 72
8. Global Markets in Action, ... 82
9. Externalities: Pollution, Education, and Health Care, ... 91
10. Production and Cost, ... 101
11. Perfect Competition, ... 112
12. Monopoly, ... 124
13. Monopolistic Competition and Oligopoly, ... 136
14. GDP: A Measure of Total Production and Income, ... 149
15. Jobs and Unemployment, ... 165
16. The CPI and the Cost of Living, ... 173
17. Potential GDP and Economic Growth, ... 183
18. Money and the Monetary System, ... 197
19. Aggregate Supply and Aggregate Demand, ... 212
20. Fiscal Policy and Monetary Policy, ... 227

1. Getting Started,

CHAPTER OUTLINE: KEY TERMS, PEOPLE, PLACES, CONCEPTS

- Scarcity
- Good
- Goods and services
- Macroeconomic
- Self-interest
- Globalization
- Information Age
- Information revolution
- Climate change
- Service
- Opportunity cost
- Hong
- Rational choice
- Choice
- Margin
- Marginal cost
- Incentive
- Correlation
- Economic model
- Scientific method
- Unemployment

1. Getting Started,
CHAPTER OUTLINE: KEY TERMS, PEOPLE, PLACES, CONCEPTS

_____ | Normative statement
_____ | Positive statement
_____ | Wealth
_____ | Wealth of Nations
_____ | Economic growth
_____ | Economics
_____ | Business cycle
_____ | Social Security
_____ | Economic policy
_____ | Policy
_____ | Cost-push inflation
_____ | Circular flow
_____ | Cost
_____ | Inflation
_____ | Origin
_____ | Variable
_____ | Scatter diagram
_____ | Trends
_____ | Linear relationship
_____ | Negative relationship
_____ | Point

1. Getting Started,

CHAPTER OUTLINE: KEY TERMS, PEOPLE, PLACES, CONCEPTS

	Ceteris paribus

CHAPTER HIGHLIGHTS & NOTES: KEY TERMS, PEOPLE, PLACES, CONCEPTS

Scarcity	Scarcity is the fundamental economic problem of having seemingly unlimited human wants in a world of limited resources. It states that society has insufficient productive resources to fulfill all human wants and needs. Additionally, scarcity implies that not all of society's goals can be pursued at the same time; trade-offs are made of one good against others.
Good	In economics, a good is a material that satisfies human wants and provides utility, for example, to a consumer making a purchase. A common distinction is made between 'goods' that are tangible property (also called goods) and services, which are non-physical. Commodities may be used as a synonym for economic goods but often refer to marketable raw materials and primary products.
Goods and services	In economics, goods and services are the outcome of human efforts to meet the wants and needs of people. Economic output is divided into physical goods and intangible services. Goods are items that can be seen and touched, such as books, pens, salt, shoes, hats, and folders.
Macroeconomic	Macroeconomics is a branch of economics dealing with the performance, structure, behavior, and decision-making of an economy as a whole, rather than individual markets. This includes national, regional, and global economies. With microeconomics, macroeconomics is one of the two most general fields in economics.
Self-interest	Self-interest generally refers to a focus on the needs or desires of the self. A number of philosophical, psychological, and economic theories examine the role of self-interest in motivating human action.
Globalization	Globaliization is the process of integration across world-space arising from the interchange of world views, products, ideas, and other aspects of culture. Advances in transportation and telecommunications infrastructure, including the rise of the telegraph and its posterity the Internet, are major factors in globalization, generating further interdependence of economic and cultural activities. Though scholars place the origins of globalization in modern times, others trace its history long before the European age of discovery and voyages to the New World.

1. Getting Started,

CHAPTER HIGHLIGHTS & NOTES: KEY TERMS, PEOPLE, PLACES, CONCEPTS

Information Age	The Information Age is a period in human history characterized by the shift from traditional industry that the industrial revolution brought through industrialization, to an economy based on information computerization. The onset of the Information Age is associated with the Digital Revolution, just as the Industrial Revolution marked the onset of the Industrial Age. During the information age, the phenomenon is that the digital industry creates a knowledge-based society surrounded by a high-tech global economy that spans over its influence on how the manufacturing throughput and the service sector operate in an efficient and convenient way.
Information revolution	The term information revolution describes current economic, social and technological trends beyond the Industrial Revolution. Many competing terms have been proposed that focus on different aspects of this societal development. The British polymath crystallographer J. D. Bernal (1939) introduced the term 'scientific and technical revolution' in his book The Social Function of Science to describe the new role that science and technology are coming to play within society.
Climate change	Climate change is a significant and lasting change in the statistical distribution of weather patterns over periods ranging from decades to millions of years. It may be a change in average weather conditions, or in the distribution of weather around the average conditions (i.e., more or fewer extreme weather events). Climate change is caused by factors such as biotic processes, variations in solar radiation received by Earth, plate tectonics, and volcanic eruptions.
Service	In economics, a service is an intangible commodity. That is, services are an example of intangible economic goods. Service provision is often an economic activity where the buyer does not generally, except by exclusive contract, obtain exclusive ownership of the thing purchased.
Opportunity cost	In microeconomic theory, the opportunity cost of a choice is the value of the best alternative forgone, in a situation in which a choice needs to be made between several mutually exclusive alternatives given limited resources. Assuming the best choice is made, it is the 'cost' incurred by not enjoying the benefit that would be had by taking the second best choice available. The New Oxford American Dictionary defines it as 'the loss of potential gain from other alternatives when one alternative is chosen'.
Hong	The Hongs were major business houses in Canton, China and later Hong Kong with significant influence on patterns of consumerism, trade, manufacturing and other key areas of the economy. They were originally led by Howqua as head of the cohong.
Rational choice	Rational choice theory, also known as choice theory or rational action theory, is a framework for understanding and often formally modeling social and economic behavior.

1. Getting Started,

CHAPTER HIGHLIGHTS & NOTES: KEY TERMS, PEOPLE, PLACES, CONCEPTS

	Rationality, interpreted as 'wanting more rather than less of a good', is widely used as an assumption of the behavior of individuals in microeconomic models and analysis and appears in almost all economics textbook treatments of human decision-making. It is also central to some of modern political science, sociology, and philosophy.
Choice	Choice consists of a mental decision, of judging the merits of multiple options and selecting one or more of them. While a choice can be made between imagined options , often a choice is made between real options and followed by the corresponding action. For example, a route for a journey is chosen based on the preference of arriving at a given destination as soon as possible.
Margin	In finance, a margin is collateral that the holder of a financial instrument has to deposit to cover some or all of the credit risk of their counterparty . This risk can arise if the holder has done any of the following:•Borrowed cash from the counterparty to buy financial instruments,•Sold financial instruments short, or•Entered into a derivative contract. The collateral can be in the form of cash or securities, and it is deposited in a margin account. On United States futures exchanges, margins were formerly called performance bonds.
Marginal cost	In economics and finance, marginal cost is the change in the total cost that arises when the quantity produced has an increment by unit. That is, it is the cost of producing one more unit of a good. In general terms, marginal cost at each level of production includes any additional costs required to produce the next unit.
Incentive	An incentive is something that motivates an individual to perform an action. The study of incentive structures is central to the study of all economic activities (both in terms of individual decision-making and in terms of co-operation and competition within a larger institutional structure). Economic analysis, then, of the differences between societies (and between different organizations within a society) largely amounts to characterizing the differences in incentive structures faced by individuals involved in these collective efforts.
Correlation	In statistics, dependence is any statistical relationship between two random variables or two sets of data. Correlation refers to any of a broad class of statistical relationships involving dependence. Familiar examples of dependent phenomena include the correlation between the physical statures of parents and their offspring, and the correlation between the demand for a product and its price.
Economic model	In economics, a model is a theoretical construct representing economic processes by a set of variables and a set of logical and/or quantitative relationships between them. The economic model is a simplified framework designed to illustrate complex processes, often but not always using mathematical techniques. Frequently, economic models posit structural parameters.

1. Getting Started,

CHAPTER HIGHLIGHTS & NOTES: KEY TERMS, PEOPLE, PLACES, CONCEPTS

Scientific method	The scientific method is a body of techniques for investigating phenomena, acquiring new knowledge, or correcting and integrating previous knowledge. To be termed scientific, a method of inquiry must be based on empirical and measurable evidence subject to specific principles of reasoning. The Oxford English Dictionary defines the scientific method as: 'a method or procedure that has characterized natural science since the 17th century, consisting in systematic observation, measurement, and experiment, and the formulation, testing, and modification of hypotheses.' The chief characteristic which distinguishes the scientific method from other methods of acquiring knowledge is that scientists seek to let reality speak for itself, supporting a theory when a theory's predictions are confirmed and challenging a theory when its predictions prove false.
Unemployment	Unemployment occurs when people are without work and actively seeking work. The unemployment rate is a measure of the prevalence of unemployment and it is calculated as a percentage by dividing the number of unemployed individuals by all individuals currently in the labor force. During periods of recession, an economy usually experiences a relatively high unemployment rate.
Normative statement	In economics, a normative statement expresses a value judgement about whether a situation is subjectively desirable or undesirable. 'The world would be a better place if the moon were made of green cheese' is a normative statement because it expresses a judgement about what ought to be. Notice that there is no way of testing the veracity of the statement; even if you disagree with it, you have no sure way of proving to someone who believes the statement that he or she is wrong by mere appeal to facts.
Positive statement	In economics and philosophy, a positive statement concerns what 'is', 'was', or 'will be', and contains no indication of approval or disapproval . Positive statements are testable - or, at least, it is possible to imagine facts that disprove them - but can be factually incorrect: 'The moon is made of black and gold cheese' is empirically false, but is still a positive statement, as it is a statement about what is, not what should be. Positive statements are contrasted with normative statements, which do make value judgements.
Wealth	The modern understanding of Wealth is the abundance of valuable resources or material possessions. This excludes the core meaning as held in the originating old English word weal, which is from an Indo-European word stem. In this larger understanding of wealth, an individual, community, region or country that possesses an abundance of such possessions or resources to the benefit of the common good is known as wealthy.
Wealth of Nations	An Inquiry into the Nature and Causes of the Wealth of Nations, generally referred to by its shortened title The Wealth of Nations, is the magnum opus of the Scottish economist and moral philosopher Adam Smith. First published in 1776, the book offers one of the world's first collected descriptions of what builds nations' wealth and is today a fundamental work in classical economics.

1. Getting Started,

CHAPTER HIGHLIGHTS & NOTES: KEY TERMS, PEOPLE, PLACES, CONCEPTS

Economic growth	Economic growth is the increase in the market value of the goods and services produced by an economy over time. It is conventionally measured as the percent rate of increase in real gross domestic product, or real GDP. Of more importance is the growth of the ratio of GDP to population (GDP per capita), which is also called per capita income. An increase in per capita income is referred to as intensive growth.
Economics	Economics is the social science that studies the behavior of individuals, groups, and organizations, when they manage or use scarce resources, which have alternative uses, to achieve desired ends. Agents are assumed to act rationally, have multiple desirable ends in sight, limited resources to obtain these ends, a set of stable preferences, a definite overall guiding objective, and the capability of making a choice. There exists an economic problem, subject to study by economic science, when a decision (choice) has to be made by one or more resource-controlling players to attain the best possible outcome under bounded rational conditions.
Business cycle	The term business cycle refers to economy-wide fluctuations in production, trade and economic activity in general over several months or years in an economy organized on free-enterprise principles. The business cycle is the upward and downward movements of levels of GDP (gross domestic product) and refers to the period of expansions and contractions in the level of economic activities (business fluctuations) around its long-term growth trend. These fluctuations occur around a long-term growth trend, and typically involve shifts over time between periods of relatively rapid economic growth (an expansion or boom), and periods of relative stagnation or decline (a contraction or recession).
Social Security	In the United States, Social Security is primarily the Old-Age, Survivors, and Disability Insurance federal program. The original Social Security Act (1935) and the current version of the Act, as amended, encompass several social welfare and social insurance programs. Social Security is funded through payroll taxes called Federal Insurance Contributions Act tax (FICA) and/or Self Employed Contributions Act Tax (SECA).
Economic policy	Economic policy refers to the actions that governments take in the economic field. It covers the systems for setting interest rates and government budget as well as the labor market, national ownership, and many other areas of government interventions into the economy. Such policies are often influenced by international institutions like the International Monetary Fund or World Bank as well as political beliefs and the consequent policies of parties.
Policy	A policy is a principle or protocol to guide decisions and achieve rational outcomes. A policy is a statement of intent, and is implemented as a procedure or protocol.

1. Getting Started,

CHAPTER HIGHLIGHTS & NOTES: KEY TERMS, PEOPLE, PLACES, CONCEPTS

Cost-push inflation	Cost-push inflation is an alleged type of inflation caused by substantial increases in the cost of important goods or services where no suitable alternative is available. A situation that has been often cited of this was the oil crisis of the 1970s, which some economists see as a major cause of the inflation experienced in the Western world in that decade. It is argued that this inflation resulted from increases in the cost of petroleum imposed by the member states of OPEC. Since petroleum is so important to industrialised economies, a large increase in its price can lead to the increase in the price of most products, raising the inflation rate.
Circular flow	In economics, the terms circular flow of income or circular flow refer to a simple economic model which describes the reciprocal circulation of income between producers and consumers. In the circular flow model, the inter-dependent entities of producer and consumer are referred to as 'firms' and 'households' respectively and provide each other with factors in order to facilitate the flow of income. Firms provide consumers with goods and services in exchange for consumer expenditure and 'factors of production' from households.
Cost	In production, research, retail, and accounting, a cost is the value of money that has been used up to produce something, and hence is not available for use anymore. In business, the cost may be one of acquisition, in which case the amount of money expended to acquire it is counted as cost. In this case, money is the input that is gone in order to acquire the thing.
Inflation	In economics, inflation is a sustained increase in the general price level of goods and services in an economy over a period of time. When the general price level rises, each unit of currency buys fewer goods and services. Consequently, inflation reflects a reduction in the purchasing power per unit of money - a loss of real value in the medium of exchange and unit of account within the economy.
Origin	Origin is a proprietary computer program for interactive scientific graphing and data analysis. It is produced by OriginLab Corporation, and runs on Microsoft Windows. It has inspired several platform-independent open-source clones like QtiPlot or SciDAVis.
Variable	In elementary mathematics, a variable is an alphabetic character representing a number which is either arbitrary or not fully specified or unknown. Making algebraic computations with variables as if they were explicit numbers allows one to solve a range of problems in a single computation. A typical example is the quadratic formula, which allows to solve every quadratic equation by simply substituting the numeric values of the coefficients of the given equation to the variables that represent them.
Scatter diagram	A scatter plot, scatterplot, or scattergraph is a type of mathematical diagram using Cartesian coordinates to display values for two variables for a set of data.

1. Getting Started,

CHAPTER HIGHLIGHTS & NOTES: KEY TERMS, PEOPLE, PLACES, CONCEPTS

	The data is displayed as a collection of points, each having the value of one variable determining the position on the horizontal axis and the value of the other variable determining the position on the vertical axis. This kind of plot is also called a scatter chart, scattergram, scatter diagram, or scatter graph.
Trends	Trends is a society, philanthropy, fashion and lifestyle magazine published in Arizona. Created by Danny Medina in 1982, it was purchased by Bill Dougherty in 2001, who now serves as its publisher. Trends has a 501(c)(3) arm, the Trends Charitable Fund (TCF), which raises money for underserved women's and children's charitable organizations.
Linear relationship	In statistics, dependence or association is any statistical relationship, whether causal or not, between two random variables or two sets of data. Correlation is any of a broad class of statistical relationships involving dependence, though in common usage it most often refers to the extent to which two variables have a linear relationship with each other. Familiar examples of dependent phenomena include the correlation between the physical statures of parents and their offspring, and the correlation between the demand for a product and its price.
Negative relationship	In statistics, a relationship between two variables is negative if the slope in a corresponding graph is negative, or--what is in some contexts equivalent--if the correlation between them is negative. Negative correlation is also variously called anti-correlation or inverse correlation. Example: 'They observed a negative relationship between illness and vaccination.' As incident of vaccination is increasing, incidence of illness is decreasing, and vice versa.
Point	Points, sometimes also called 'discount points', are a form of pre-paid interest. One point equals one percent of the loan amount. By charging a borrower points, a lender effectively increases the yield on the loan above the amount of the stated interest rate.
Ceteris paribus	Ceteris paribus or caeteris paribus is a Latin phrase meaning 'with other things the same' or 'all other things being equal or held constant.' As an ablative absolute, it is commonly posed to mean 'all other things being equal.' A prediction or a statement about causal, empirical, or logical relation between two states of affairs is ceteris paribus via acknowledgement that the prediction can fail or the relation can be abolished by intervening factors. A ceteris paribus assumption is often key to scientific inquiry, as scientists seek to screen out factors that perturb a relation of interest.

1. Getting Started,

CHAPTER QUIZ: KEY TERMS, PEOPLE, PLACES, CONCEPTS

1. In economics, _____ are the outcome of human efforts to meet the wants and needs of people. Economic output is divided into physical goods and intangible services. Goods are items that can be seen and touched, such as books, pens, salt, shoes, hats, and folders.

    a. Consumables
    b. Goods and services
    c. Port centric logistics
    d. Work in process

2. _____ is a significant and lasting change in the statistical distribution of weather patterns over periods ranging from decades to millions of years. It may be a change in average weather conditions, or in the distribution of weather around the average conditions (i.e., more or fewer extreme weather events). _____ is caused by factors such as biotic processes, variations in solar radiation received by Earth, plate tectonics, and volcanic eruptions.

    a. Bangladesh climate Multi Donor Trust Fund
    b. Climate change
    c. Carbon credit
    d. Carbon finance

3. In finance, a _____ is collateral that the holder of a financial instrument has to deposit to cover some or all of the credit risk of their counterparty. This risk can arise if the holder has done any of the following:•Borrowed cash from the counterparty to buy financial instruments,•Sold financial instruments short, or•Entered into a derivative contract.

    The collateral can be in the form of cash or securities, and it is deposited in a _____ account. On United States futures exchanges, _____s were formerly called performance bonds.

    a. Bid price
    b. Big Bang
    c. Margin
    d. Block trade

4. _____ is the fundamental economic problem of having seemingly unlimited human wants in a world of limited resources. It states that society has insufficient productive resources to fulfill all human wants and needs. Additionally, _____ implies that not all of society's goals can be pursued at the same time; trade-offs are made of one good against others.

    a. Grain trade
    b. Grain supply to the city of Rome
    c. Scarcity
    d. Corn exchange

5. . In economics, a _____ is a material that satisfies human wants and provides utility, for example, to a consumer making a purchase. A common distinction is made between '_____s' that are tangible property (also called _____s) and services, which are non-physical.

1. Getting Started,

CHAPTER QUIZ: KEY TERMS, PEOPLE, PLACES, CONCEPTS

Commodities may be used as a synonym for economic _____s but often refer to marketable raw materials and primary products.

a. Cigar Box Method
b. Common Agricultural Policy
c. Good
d. Cash crop

ANSWER KEY
1. Getting Started,

1. b
2. b
3. c
4. c
5. c

You can take the complete Online Interactive Chapter Practice Test

for 1. Getting Started,
on all key terms, persons, places, and concepts.

No Additional Costs

http://www.Cram101.com

Register, send an email request to Travis.Reese@Cram101.com to get your user Id and password.

Include your customer order number, and ISBN number from your studyguide Retailer.

2. The U.S. and Global Economies,

CHAPTER OUTLINE: KEY TERMS, PEOPLE, PLACES, CONCEPTS

	Capital good
	Consumption
	Capital
	Good
	Service
	Economy
	Income
	Production
	Factor
	Factors of production
	Gift
	Hong
	Land
	Natural monopoly
	Product differentiation
	Economic growth
	Natural resource
	Executive officer
	Financial capital
	Human capital
	Information Age

2. The U.S. and Global Economies,
CHAPTER OUTLINE: KEY TERMS, PEOPLE, PLACES, CONCEPTS

- _____ Entrepreneurship
- _____ Information
- _____ Information economy
- _____ Rate
- _____ Interest
- _____ Profit
- _____ Wage
- _____ Distribution
- _____ Standard of living
- _____ BRICS
- _____ Goods and services
- _____ Index
- _____ Market
- _____ Nature
- _____ Price index
- _____ Economic policy
- _____ Physical capital
- _____ Policy
- _____ Income distribution
- _____ Poverty
- _____ Average

2. The U.S. and Global Economies,

CHAPTER OUTLINE: KEY TERMS, PEOPLE, PLACES, CONCEPTS

| Average income
| Cost
| Fixed cost
| Post-industrial economy
| Choice
| Business cycle
| Circular flow
| Factor market
| Household
| Import
| Theory
| Google
| Social Security
| State government
| Welfare
| Export
| International finance
| International trade
| Outsourcing
| Trade

2. The U.S. and Global Economies,

CHAPTER HIGHLIGHTS & NOTES: KEY TERMS, PEOPLE, PLACES, CONCEPTS

Capital good	A capital good is a durable good that is used in the production of goods or services. Capital goods are one of the three types of producer goods, the other two being land and labor, which are also known collectively as primary factors of production. This classification originated during the classical economic period and has remained the dominant method for classification.
Consumption	Consumption is a major concept in economics and is also studied by many other social sciences. Economists are particularly interested in the relationship between consumption and income, and therefore in economics the consumption function plays a major role. Different schools of economists define production and consumption differently.
Capital	In economics, capital goods, real capital, or capital assets are already-produced durable goods or any non-financial asset that is used in production of goods or services. Capital goods are not significantly consumed in the production process though they may depreciate. How a capital good or is maintained or returned to its pre-production state varies with the type of capital involved.
Good	In economics, a good is a material that satisfies human wants and provides utility, for example, to a consumer making a purchase. A common distinction is made between 'goods' that are tangible property (also called goods) and services, which are non-physical. Commodities may be used as a synonym for economic goods but often refer to marketable raw materials and primary products.
Service	In economics, a service is an intangible commodity. That is, services are an example of intangible economic goods. Service provision is often an economic activity where the buyer does not generally, except by exclusive contract, obtain exclusive ownership of the thing purchased.
Economy	An economy or economic system consists of the production, distribution or trade, and consumption of limited goods and services by different agents in a given geographical location. The economic agents can be individuals, businesses, organizations, or governments. Transactions occur when two parties agree to the value or price of the transacted good or service, commonly expressed in a certain currency.
Income	Income is the consumption and savings opportunity gained by an entity within a specified timeframe, which is generally expressed in monetary terms. However, for households and individuals, 'income is the sum of all the wages, salaries, profits, interests payments, rents and other forms of earnings received... in a given period of time.' In the field of public economics, the term may refer to the accumulation of both monetary and non-monetary consumption ability, with the former (monetary) being used as a proxy for total income.

2. The U.S. and Global Economies,

CHAPTER HIGHLIGHTS & NOTES: KEY TERMS, PEOPLE, PLACES, CONCEPTS

Production	Production is a process of combining various material inputs and immaterial inputs in order to make something for consumption (the output). It is the act of creating output, a good or service which has value and contributes to the utility of individuals. Economic well-being is created in a production process, meaning all economic activities that aim directly or indirectly to satisfy human needs.
Factor	A factor, Latin for 'doer, maker', is a mercantile fiduciary who receives and sells goods on commission (called factorage), transacting business in his own name and not disclosing his principal, and historically with his seat at a factory (trading post). A factor differs from a commission merchant in that a factor takes possession of goods (or documents of title representing goods) on consignment, whereas a commission merchant sells goods not in his possession on the basis of samples. Most modern factor business is in the textile field, but factors are also used to a great extent in the shoe, furniture, hardware, and other industries, and the trade areas in which factors operate have increased.
Factors of production	In economics, factors of production are the inputs to the production process. Finished goods are the output. Input determines the quantity of output i.e. output depends upon input.
Gift	A gift, in the law of property, is the voluntary transfer of property from one person to another (the donee or grantee) without full valuable consideration. In order for a gift to be legally effective, the donor must have intended to give the gift to the donee (donative intent), and the gift must actually be delivered to and accepted by the donee. Gifts can be either:•lifetime gifts (inter vivos gift, donatio inter vivos) - a gift of a present or future interest made and delivered in the donor's lifetime; or•deathbed gifts (gift causa mortis, donatio mortis causa) - a future gift made in expectation of the donor's imminent death.
Hong	The Hongs were major business houses in Canton, China and later Hong Kong with significant influence on patterns of consumerism, trade, manufacturing and other key areas of the economy. They were originally led by Howqua as head of the cohong.
Land	In economics, land comprises all naturally occurring resources whose supply is inherently fixed. Examples are any and all particular geographical locations, mineral deposits, and even geostationary orbit locations and portions of the electromagnetic spectrum. Natural resources are fundamental to the production of all goods, including capital goods.
Natural monopoly	A monopoly is a firm which is the only one producing and selling a particular product. A natural monopoly is a monopoly in an industry in which it is most efficient (involving the lowest long-run average cost) for production to be concentrated in a single firm. This market situation gives the largest supplier in an industry, often the first supplier in a market, an overwhelming cost advantage over other actual and potential competitors, so a natural monopoly situation generally leads to an actual monopoly.

2. The U.S. and Global Economies,

CHAPTER HIGHLIGHTS & NOTES: KEY TERMS, PEOPLE, PLACES, CONCEPTS

Product differentiation	In economics and marketing, product differentiation is the process of distinguishing a product or service from others, to make it more attractive to a particular target market. This involves differentiating it from competitors' products as well as a firm's own products. The concept was proposed by Edward Chamberlin in his 1933 Theory of Monopolistic Competition.
Economic growth	Economic growth is the increase in the market value of the goods and services produced by an economy over time. It is conventionally measured as the percent rate of increase in real gross domestic product, or real GDP. Of more importance is the growth of the ratio of GDP to population (GDP per capita), which is also called per capita income. An increase in per capita income is referred to as intensive growth.
Natural resource	Natural resources are resources that exist without actions of humankind. This includes all valued characteristics such as magnetic, gravitational, and electrical properties and forces. On earth it includes; sunlight, atmosphere, water, land, air (includes all minerals) along with all vegetation and animal life that naturally subsists upon or within the heretofore identified characteristics and substances.
Executive officer	An executive officer is generally a person responsible for running an organization, although the exact nature of the role varies depending on the organization.
Financial capital	Financial capital is money used by entrepreneurs and businesses to buy what they need to make their products or to provide their services to the sector of the economy upon which their operation is based, i.e. retail, corporate, investment banking, etc.
Human capital	Human capital is the stock of knowledge, habits, social and personality attributes, including creativity, embodied in the ability to perform labor so as to produce economic value. Alternatively, Human capital is a collection of resources--all the knowledge, talents, skills, abilities, experience, intelligence, training, judgment, and wisdom possessed individually and collectively by individuals in a population.
Information Age	The Information Age is a period in human history characterized by the shift from traditional industry that the industrial revolution brought through industrialization, to an economy based on information computerization. The onset of the Information Age is associated with the Digital Revolution, just as the Industrial Revolution marked the onset of the Industrial Age. During the information age, the phenomenon is that the digital industry creates a knowledge-based society surrounded by a high-tech global economy that spans over its influence on how the manufacturing throughput and the service sector operate in an efficient and convenient way.

2. The U.S. and Global Economies,

CHAPTER HIGHLIGHTS & NOTES: KEY TERMS, PEOPLE, PLACES, CONCEPTS

Entrepreneurship	In political economics, entrepreneurship is the process of identifying and starting a business venture, sourcing and organizing the required resources and taking both the risks and rewards associated with the venture.
Information	Information is that which informs, i.e., that from which data can be derived. Information is conveyed either as the content of a message or through direct or indirect observation of some thing. That which is perceived can be construed as a message in its own right, and in that sense, information is always conveyed as the content of a message.
Information economy	Information economy is an economy with an increased emphasis on informational activities and information industry. Manuel Castells states that information economy is not mutually exclusive with manufacturing economy. He finds that some countries such as Germany and Japan exhibit the informatization of manufacturing processes.
Rate	In mathematics, a rate is a ratio between two measurements with different units. If the unit or quantity in respect of which something is changing is not specified, usually the rate is per unit time. However, a rate of change can be specified per unit time, or per unit of length or mass or another quantity.
Interest	Interest is a fee paid by a borrower of assets to the owner as a form of compensation for the use of the assets. It is most commonly the price paid for the use of borrowed money, or money earned by deposited funds. When money is borrowed, interest is typically paid to the lender as a percentage of the principal, the amount owed to the lender.
Profit	In neoclassical microeconomic theory, the term profit has two related but distinct meanings. Economic profit is similar to accounting profit but smaller because it reflects the total opportunity costs (both explicit and implicit) of a venture to an investor. Normal profit refers to a situation in which the economic profit is zero.
Wage	A wage is monetary compensation paid by an employer to an employee in exchange for work done. Payment may be calculated as a fixed amount for each task completed (a task wage or piece rate), or at an hourly or daily rate, or based on an easily measured quantity of work done. Payment by wage contrasts with salaried work, in which the employer pays an arranged amount at steady intervals (such as a week or month) regardless of hours worked, with commission which conditions pay on individual performance, and with compensation based on the performance of the company as a whole.

2. The U.S. and Global Economies,

CHAPTER HIGHLIGHTS & NOTES: KEY TERMS, PEOPLE, PLACES, CONCEPTS

Distribution	The Dagum distribution is a continuous probability distribution defined over all positive real numbers. It is named after Camilo Dagum, who proposed it in a series of papers in the 1970s. The Dagum distribution arose from several variants of a new model on the size distribution of personal income and is mostly associated with the study of income distribution.
Standard of living	Standard of living refers to the level of wealth, comfort, material goods and necessities available to a certain socioeconomic class in a certain geographic area. The standard of living includes factors such as income, quality and availability of employment, class disparity, poverty rate, quality and affordability of housing, hours of work required to purchase necessities, gross domestic product, inflation rate, number of holiday days per year, affordable (or free) access to quality healthcare, quality and availability of education, life expectancy, incidence of disease, cost of goods and services, infrastructure, national economic growth, economic and political and stability, political and religious freedom, environmental quality, climate and safety. The standard of living is closely related to quality of life.
BRICS	BRICS is the acronym for an association of five major emerging national economies: Brazil, Russia, India, China and South Africa. The grouping was originally known as 'BRIC' before the inclusion of South Africa in 2010. The BRICS members are all developing or newly industrialised countries, but they are distinguished by their large, fast-growing economies and significant influence on regional and global affairs; all five are G-20 members. As of 2013, the five BRICS countries represent almost 3 billion people, with a combined nominal GDP of US$16.039 trillion, and an estimated US$4 trillion in combined foreign reserves. Presently, South Africa holds the chair of the BRICS group, having hosted the group's fifth summit in 2013. The BRICS have received both praise and criticism from numerous quarters.
Goods and services	In economics, goods and services are the outcome of human efforts to meet the wants and needs of people. Economic output is divided into physical goods and intangible services. Goods are items that can be seen and touched, such as books, pens, salt, shoes, hats, and folders.
Index	In economics and finance, an index is a statistical measure of changes in a representative group of individual data points. These data may be derived from any number of sources, including company performance, prices, productivity, and employment. Economic indices (index, plural) track economic health from different perspectives.
Market	A market is one of the many varieties of systems, institutions, procedures, social relations and infrastructures whereby parties engage in exchange. While parties may exchange goods and services by barter, most markets rely on sellers offering their goods or services (including labor) in exchange for money from buyers. It can be said that a market is the process by which the prices of goods and services are established.

2. The U.S. and Global Economies,

CHAPTER HIGHLIGHTS & NOTES: KEY TERMS, PEOPLE, PLACES, CONCEPTS

Nature	Nature is a concept with two major sets of inter-related meanings, referring on the one hand to the things which are natural, or subject to the normal working of 'laws of nature', or on the other hand to the essential properties and causes of those things to be what they naturally are, or in other words the laws of nature themselves.
	How to understand the meaning and significance of nature has been a consistent theme of discussion within the history of Western Civilization, in the philosophical fields of metaphysics and epistemology, as well as in theology and science. The study of natural things and the regular laws which seem to govern them, as opposed to discussion about what it means to be natural, is the area of natural science.
Price index	A price index is a normalized average of price relatives for a given class of goods or services in a given region, during a given interval of time. It is a statistic designed to help to compare how these price relatives, taken as a whole, differ between time periods or geographical locations.
	Price indexes have several potential uses.
Economic policy	Economic policy refers to the actions that governments take in the economic field. It covers the systems for setting interest rates and government budget as well as the labor market, national ownership, and many other areas of government interventions into the economy.
	Such policies are often influenced by international institutions like the International Monetary Fund or World Bank as well as political beliefs and the consequent policies of parties.
Physical capital	In economics, physical capital or just 'capital' refers to a factor of production, such as machinery, buildings, or computers. The production function takes the general form $Y=f(K, L)$, where Y is output, K is capital stock and L is labor. In economic theory, physical capital is one of the three primary factors of production, also known as inputs production function.
Policy	A policy is a principle or protocol to guide decisions and achieve rational outcomes. A policy is a statement of intent, and is implemented as a procedure or protocol. Policies are generally adopted by the Board of or senior governance body within an organization whereas procedures or protocols would be developed and adopted by senior executive officers.
Income distribution	In economics, income distribution is how a nation's total GDP is distributed amongst its population.
	Income and distribution has always been a central concern of economic theory and economic policy. Classical economists such as Adam Smith, Thomas Malthus and David Ricardo were mainly concerned with factor income distribution, that is, the distribution of income between the main factors of production, land, labour and capital.

2. The U.S. and Global Economies,

CHAPTER HIGHLIGHTS & NOTES: KEY TERMS, PEOPLE, PLACES, CONCEPTS

Poverty	Poverty is general scarcity or dearth, or the state of one who lacks a certain amount of material possessions or money. Absolute poverty or destitution refers to the deprivation of basic human needs, which commonly includes food, water, sanitation, clothing, shelter, health care and education. Relative poverty is defined contextually as economic inequality in the location or society in which people live.
Average	In colloquial language average usually refers to the sum of a list of numbers divided by the size of the list, in other words the arithmetic mean. However, the word 'average' can be used to refer to the median, the mode, or some other central or typical value. In statistics, these are all known as measures of central tendency.
Average income	Per capita income or average income measures the average income earned per person in a given area in a specified year. It is calculated by dividing the area's total income by its total population.
Cost	In production, research, retail, and accounting, a cost is the value of money that has been used up to produce something, and hence is not available for use anymore. In business, the cost may be one of acquisition, in which case the amount of money expended to acquire it is counted as cost. In this case, money is the input that is gone in order to acquire the thing.
Fixed cost	In economics, fixed costs, indirect costs or overheads are business expenses that are not dependent on the level of goods or services produced by the business. They tend to be time-related, such as salaries or rents being paid per month, and are often referred to as overhead costs. This is in contrast to variable costs, which are volume-related (and are paid per quantity produced).
Post-industrial economy	A post-industrial economy refers to a period of growth within an industrialized economy or nation in which the relative importance of manufacturing lessens and that of services, information, and research grows. Such economies are often marked by:•A declining manufacturing sector, resulting in deindustrialization,•a large service sector, and•an increase in the amount of information technology, often leading to an 'information age'. Information, knowledge, and creativity are the new raw materials of such an economy. The industry aspect of a post-industrial economy is sent into less developed nations which manufacture what is needed at lower costs .
Choice	Choice consists of a mental decision, of judging the merits of multiple options and selecting one or more of them. While a choice can be made between imagined options , often a choice is made between real options and followed by the corresponding action. For example, a route for a journey is chosen based on the preference of arriving at a given destination as soon as possible.

2. The U.S. and Global Economies,

CHAPTER HIGHLIGHTS & NOTES: KEY TERMS, PEOPLE, PLACES, CONCEPTS

Business cycle	The term business cycle refers to economy-wide fluctuations in production, trade and economic activity in general over several months or years in an economy organized on free-enterprise principles. The business cycle is the upward and downward movements of levels of GDP (gross domestic product) and refers to the period of expansions and contractions in the level of economic activities (business fluctuations) around its long-term growth trend. These fluctuations occur around a long-term growth trend, and typically involve shifts over time between periods of relatively rapid economic growth (an expansion or boom), and periods of relative stagnation or decline (a contraction or recession).
Circular flow	In economics, the terms circular flow of income or circular flow refer to a simple economic model which describes the reciprocal circulation of income between producers and consumers. In the circular flow model, the inter-dependent entities of producer and consumer are referred to as 'firms' and 'households' respectively and provide each other with factors in order to facilitate the flow of income. Firms provide consumers with goods and services in exchange for consumer expenditure and 'factors of production' from households.
Factor market	In economics a factor market refers to markets where services of the factors of production are bought and sold such as the labor markets, the capital market, the market for raw materials, and the market for management or entrepreneurial resources. Firms buy productive resources in return for making factor payments at factor prices. The interaction between product and factor markets involves the principle of derived demand.
Household	A household consists of one or more people who live in the same dwelling and also share at meals or living accommodation, and may consist of a single family or some other grouping of people. A single dwelling will be considered to contain multiple households if meals or living space are not shared. The household is the basic unit of analysis in many social, microeconomic and government models, and is important to the fields of economics, inheritance.
Import	An import is a good brought into a jurisdiction, especially across a national border, from an external source. The purchaser of the exotic good is called an importer. An import in the receiving country is an export from the sending country.
Theory	Theory is a group of ideas meant to explain a certain topic of science, such as a single or collection of fact, event(s), or phenomen(a)(on). Typically, a theory is developed through the use of contemplative and rational forms of abstract and generalized thinking. Furthermore, a theory is often based on general principles that are independent of the thing being explained.

2. The U.S. and Global Economies,

CHAPTER HIGHLIGHTS & NOTES: KEY TERMS, PEOPLE, PLACES, CONCEPTS

Google	Google is an American multinational corporation specializing in Internet-related services and products. These include search, cloud computing, software, and online advertising technologies. Most of its profits are derived from AdWords.
Social Security	In the United States, Social Security is primarily the Old-Age, Survivors, and Disability Insurance federal program. The original Social Security Act (1935) and the current version of the Act, as amended, encompass several social welfare and social insurance programs. Social Security is funded through payroll taxes called Federal Insurance Contributions Act tax (FICA) and/or Self Employed Contributions Act Tax (SECA).
State government	A state government is the government of a country subdivision in a federal form of government, which shares political power with the federal or national government. A state government may have some level of political autonomy, or be subject to the direct control of the federal government. This relationship may be defined by a constitution.
Welfare	Welfare is the provision of a minimal level of well-being and social support for all citizens, sometimes referred to as public aid. In most developed countries welfare is largely provided by the government, and to a lesser extent, charities, informal social groups, religious groups, and inter-governmental organizations. The welfare state expands on this concept to include services such as universal healthcare and unemployment insurance.
Export	The term export means shipping the goods and services out of the port of a country. The seller of such goods and services is referred to as an 'exporter' who is based in the country of export whereas the overseas based buyer is referred to as an 'importer'. In International Trade, 'exports' refers to selling goods and services produced in the home country to other markets.
International finance	International finance is the branch of financial economics broadly concerned with monetary and macroeconomic interrelations between two or more countries. International finance examines the dynamics of the global financial system, international monetary systems, balance of payments, exchange rates, foreign direct investment, and how these topics relate to international trade. Sometimes referred to as multinational finance, international finance is additionally concerned with matters of international financial management.
International trade	International trade is the exchange of capital, goods, and services across international borders or territories. In most countries, such trade represents a significant share of gross domestic product (GDP). While international trade has been present throughout much of history, its economic, social, and political importance has been on the rise in recent centuries.
Outsourcing	In business, outsourcing is the contracting out of a business process to a third-party.

2. The U.S. and Global Economies,

CHAPTER HIGHLIGHTS & NOTES: KEY TERMS, PEOPLE, PLACES, CONCEPTS

	The term 'outsourcing' became popular in the United States near the turn of the 21st century. Outsourcing sometimes involves transferring employees and assets from one firm to another, but not always.
Trade	Trade, also called goods exchange economy, is to transfer the ownership of goods from one person or entity to another by getting a product or service in exchange from the buyer. Trade is sometimes loosely called commerce or financial transaction or barter. A network that allows trade is called a market.

CHAPTER QUIZ: KEY TERMS, PEOPLE, PLACES, CONCEPTS

1. _____ consists of a mental decision, of judging the merits of multiple options and selecting one or more of them. While a _____ can be made between imagined options, often a _____ is made between real options and followed by the corresponding action. For example, a route for a journey is chosen based on the preference of arriving at a given destination as soon as possible.

   a. Behavioral operations research
   b. Belief decision matrix
   c. Belief structure
   d. Choice

2. A _____ is monetary compensation paid by an employer to an employee in exchange for work done. Payment may be calculated as a fixed amount for each task completed (a task _____ or piece rate), or at an hourly or daily rate, or based on an easily measured quantity of work done.

   Payment by _____ contrasts with salaried work, in which the employer pays an arranged amount at steady intervals (such as a week or month) regardless of hours worked, with commission which conditions pay on individual performance, and with compensation based on the performance of the company as a whole.

   a. Capital account
   b. Capital formation
   c. Wage
   d. Domar aggregation

3. . An _____ or economic system consists of the production, distribution or trade, and consumption of limited goods and services by different agents in a given geographical location. The economic agents can be individuals, businesses, organizations, or governments. Transactions occur when two parties agree to the value or price of the transacted good or service, commonly expressed in a certain currency.

   a. Care work

2. The U.S. and Global Economies,

CHAPTER QUIZ: KEY TERMS, PEOPLE, PLACES, CONCEPTS

    b. Cash collection
    c. Economy
    d. Commodity production

4. In business, _____ is the contracting out of a business process to a third-party. The term '_____' became popular in the United States near the turn of the 21st century. _____ sometimes involves transferring employees and assets from one firm to another, but not always.

    a. 2008 G-20 Washington summit
    b. Backsourcing
    c. Bimetallism
    d. Outsourcing

5. _____ is the stock of knowledge, habits, social and personality attributes, including creativity, embodied in the ability to perform labor so as to produce economic value.

    Alternatively, _____ is a collection of resources--all the knowledge, talents, skills, abilities, experience, intelligence, training, judgment, and wisdom possessed individually and collectively by individuals in a population.

    a. cohesion funds European Union
    b. Capital flight
    c. Capital formation
    d. Human capital

ANSWER KEY
2. The U.S. and Global Economies,

1. d
2. c
3. c
4. d
5. d

You can take the complete Online Interactive Chapter Practice Test

for 2. The U.S. and Global Economies,
on all key terms, persons, places, and concepts.

No Additional Costs

http://www.Cram101.com

Register, send an email request to Travis.Reese@Cram101.com to get your user Id and password.

Include your customer order number, and ISBN number from your studyguide Retailer.

3. The Economic Problem,

CHAPTER OUTLINE: KEY TERMS, PEOPLE, PLACES, CONCEPTS

	Production possibilities frontier
	Scarcity
	Industrial Revolution
	Product differentiation
	Production
	Circular flow
	Free lunch
	Consumer
	Opportunity cost
	Cost
	Resource
	Economic growth
	Hong
	Income
	Shale
	Absolute advantage
	Comparative advantage
	Productivity
	Specialization
	Trade

3. The Economic Problem,

CHAPTER HIGHLIGHTS & NOTES: KEY TERMS, PEOPLE, PLACES, CONCEPTS

Production possibilities frontier	In economics, a production-possibility frontier, sometimes called a production-possibility curve, production-possibility boundary or product transformation curve, is a graph that shows the various combinations of amounts that two commodities could produce using the same fixed total amount of each of the factors of production. Graphically bounding the production set for fixed input quantities, the production possibilities frontier curve shows the maximum possible production level of one commodity for any given production level of the other, given the existing state of technology. By doing so, it defines productive efficiency in the context of that production set: a point on the frontier indicates efficient use of the available inputs, while a point beneath the curve indicates inefficiency.
Scarcity	Scarcity is the fundamental economic problem of having seemingly unlimited human wants in a world of limited resources. It states that society has insufficient productive resources to fulfill all human wants and needs. Additionally, scarcity implies that not all of society's goals can be pursued at the same time; trade-offs are made of one good against others.
Industrial Revolution	The Industrial Revolution was the transition to new manufacturing processes in the period from about 1760 to sometime between 1820 and 1840. This transition included going from hand production methods to machines, new chemical manufacturing and iron production processes, improved efficiency of water power, the increasing use of steam power and the development of machine tools. It also included the change from wood and other bio-fuels to coal. Textiles were the dominant industry of the Industrial Revolution in terms of employment, value of output and capital invested.
Product differentiation	In economics and marketing, product differentiation is the process of distinguishing a product or service from others, to make it more attractive to a particular target market. This involves differentiating it from competitors' products as well as a firm's own products. The concept was proposed by Edward Chamberlin in his 1933 Theory of Monopolistic Competition.
Production	Production is a process of combining various material inputs and immaterial inputs in order to make something for consumption (the output). It is the act of creating output, a good or service which has value and contributes to the utility of individuals. Economic well-being is created in a production process, meaning all economic activities that aim directly or indirectly to satisfy human needs.
Circular flow	In economics, the terms circular flow of income or circular flow refer to a simple economic model which describes the reciprocal circulation of income between producers and consumers. In the circular flow model, the inter-dependent entities of producer and consumer are referred to as 'firms' and 'households' respectively and provide each other with factors in order to facilitate the flow of income. Firms provide consumers with goods and services in exchange for consumer expenditure and 'factors of production' from households.
Free lunch	A free lunch is a sales enticement that offers a meal at no cost in order to attract customers and increase revenues from other offerings.

3. The Economic Problem,

CHAPTER HIGHLIGHTS & NOTES: KEY TERMS, PEOPLE, PLACES, CONCEPTS

	It was a tradition once common in saloons in many places in the United States, with the phrase appearing in U.S. literature from about 1870 to 1920. These establishments included a 'free' lunch, varying from rudimentary to quite elaborate, with the purchase of at least one drink. These free lunches were typically worth far more than the price of a single drink.
Consumer	A consumer is a person or group of people, such as a household, who are the final users of products or services. The consumer's use is final in the sense that the product is usually not improved by the use.
Opportunity cost	In microeconomic theory, the opportunity cost of a choice is the value of the best alternative forgone, in a situation in which a choice needs to be made between several mutually exclusive alternatives given limited resources. Assuming the best choice is made, it is the 'cost' incurred by not enjoying the benefit that would be had by taking the second best choice available. The New Oxford American Dictionary defines it as 'the loss of potential gain from other alternatives when one alternative is chosen'.
Cost	In production, research, retail, and accounting, a cost is the value of money that has been used up to produce something, and hence is not available for use anymore. In business, the cost may be one of acquisition, in which case the amount of money expended to acquire it is counted as cost. In this case, money is the input that is gone in order to acquire the thing.
Resource	A resource is a source or supply from which benefit is produced. Typically resources are materials, services, staff, or other assets that are transformed to produce benefit and in the process may be consumed or made unavailable. Benefits of resource utilization may include increased wealth, meeting needs or wants, proper functioning of a system, or enhanced well being.
Economic growth	Economic growth is the increase in the market value of the goods and services produced by an economy over time. It is conventionally measured as the percent rate of increase in real gross domestic product, or real GDP. Of more importance is the growth of the ratio of GDP to population (GDP per capita), which is also called per capita income. An increase in per capita income is referred to as intensive growth.
Hong	The Hongs were major business houses in Canton, China and later Hong Kong with significant influence on patterns of consumerism, trade, manufacturing and other key areas of the economy. They were originally led by Howqua as head of the cohong.
Income	Income is the consumption and savings opportunity gained by an entity within a specified timeframe, which is generally expressed in monetary terms. However, for households and individuals, 'income is the sum of all the wages, salaries, profits, interests payments, rents and other forms of earnings received... in a given period of time.'

3. The Economic Problem,

CHAPTER HIGHLIGHTS & NOTES: KEY TERMS, PEOPLE, PLACES, CONCEPTS

	In the field of public economics, the term may refer to the accumulation of both monetary and non-monetary consumption ability, with the former (monetary) being used as a proxy for total income.
Shale	Shale is a fine-grained, clastic sedimentary rock composed of mud that is a mix of flakes of clay minerals and tiny fragments of other minerals, especially quartz and calcite. The ratio of clay to other minerals is variable. Shale is characterized by breaks along thin laminae or parallel layering or bedding less than one centimeter in thickness, called fissility.
Absolute advantage	In economics, the principle of absolute advantage refers to the ability of a party to produce more of a good or service than competitors, using the same amount of resources. Adam Smith first described the principle of absolute advantage in the context of international trade, using labor as the only input. Since absolute advantage is determined by a simple comparison of labor productivities, it is possible for a party to have no absolute advantage in anything; in that case, according to the theory of absolute advantage, no trade will occur with the other party.
Comparative advantage	In economics, comparative advantage refers to the ability of a party to produce a particular good or service at a lower marginal and opportunity cost over another. Even if one country is more efficient in the production of all goods (absolute advantage in all goods) than the other, both countries will still gain by trading with each other, as long as they have different relative efficiencies. For example, if, using machinery, a worker in one country can produce both shoes and shirts at 6 per hour, and a worker in a country with less machinery can produce either 2 shoes or 4 shirts in an hour, each country can gain from trade because their internal trade-offs between shoes and shirts are different.
Productivity	Productivity is the ratio of output to inputs in production; it is an average measure of the efficiency of production. Efficiency of production means production's capability to create incomes which is measured by the formula real output value minus real input value. Increasing national productivity can raise living standards because more real income improves people's ability to purchase goods and services, enjoy leisure, improve housing and education and contribute to social and environmental programs.
Specialization	Specialization is the separation of tasks within a system. In a multicellular creature, cells are specialized for functions such as bone construction or oxygen transport. In capitalist societies, individual workers specialize for functions such as building construction or gasoline transport.
Trade	Trade, also called goods exchange economy, is to transfer the ownership of goods from one person or entity to another by getting a product or service in exchange from the buyer.

3. The Economic Problem,

CHAPTER HIGHLIGHTS & NOTES: KEY TERMS, PEOPLE, PLACES, CONCEPTS

> Trade is sometimes loosely called commerce or financial transaction or barter. A network that allows trade is called a market.

CHAPTER QUIZ: KEY TERMS, PEOPLE, PLACES, CONCEPTS

1. _____, also called goods exchange economy, is to transfer the ownership of goods from one person or entity to another by getting a product or service in exchange from the buyer. _____ is sometimes loosely called commerce or financial transaction or barter. A network that allows _____ is called a market.

    a. Bandar Siraf
    b. California hide trade
    c. Camel train
    d. Trade

2. In economics, a production-possibility frontier, sometimes called a production-possibility curve, production-possibility boundary or product transformation curve, is a graph that shows the various combinations of amounts that two commodities could produce using the same fixed total amount of each of the factors of production. Graphically bounding the production set for fixed input quantities, the _____ curve shows the maximum possible production level of one commodity for any given production level of the other, given the existing state of technology. By doing so, it defines productive efficiency in the context of that production set: a point on the frontier indicates efficient use of the available inputs, while a point beneath the curve indicates inefficiency.

    a. Dual-beta
    b. Base period
    c. Production possibilities frontier
    d. Blanket order

3. . In economics, the principle of _____ refers to the ability of a party to produce more of a good or service than competitors, using the same amount of resources. Adam Smith first described the principle of _____ in the context of international trade, using labor as the only input.

    Since _____ is determined by a simple comparison of labor productivities, it is possible for a party to have no _____ in anything; in that case, according to the theory of _____, no trade will occur with the other party.

    a. Cigar Box Method
    b. Casa grande
    c. Cash crop

3. The Economic Problem,

CHAPTER QUIZ: KEY TERMS, PEOPLE, PLACES, CONCEPTS

4. In microeconomic theory, the _____ of a choice is the value of the best alternative forgone, in a situation in which a choice needs to be made between several mutually exclusive alternatives given limited resources. Assuming the best choice is made, it is the 'cost' incurred by not enjoying the benefit that would be had by taking the second best choice available. The New Oxford American Dictionary defines it as 'the loss of potential gain from other alternatives when one alternative is chosen'.

    a. Benefit principle
    b. Bliss point
    c. Club good
    d. Opportunity cost

5. In economics, the terms _____ of income or _____ refer to a simple economic model which describes the reciprocal circulation of income between producers and consumers. In the _____ model, the inter-dependent entities of producer and consumer are referred to as 'firms' and 'households' respectively and provide each other with factors in order to facilitate the flow of income. Firms provide consumers with goods and services in exchange for consumer expenditure and 'factors of production' from households.

    a. cohesion funds European Union
    b. Constant elasticity of substitution
    c. Circular flow
    d. Cost-of-production theory of value

ANSWER KEY
3. The Economic Problem,

1. d
2. c
3. d
4. d
5. c

You can take the complete Online Interactive Chapter Practice Test

for 3. The Economic Problem,
on all key terms, persons, places, and concepts.

No Additional Costs

http://www.Cram101.com

Register, send an email request to Travis.Reese@Cram101.com to get your user Id and password.

Include your customer order number, and ISBN number from your studyguide Retailer.

4. Demand and Supply,

CHAPTER OUTLINE: KEY TERMS, PEOPLE, PLACES, CONCEPTS

_____ Perfect competition

_____ Resource

_____ Competitive Market

_____ Demand

_____ Law of demand

_____ Demand curve

_____ Index

_____ Market

_____ Import

_____ Price

_____ Inferior good

_____ Normal good

_____ Preference

_____ Income

_____ Law of supply

_____ Supply

_____ Supply curve

_____ Product

_____ Product differentiation

_____ Price level

_____ Productivity

4. Demand and Supply,
CHAPTER OUTLINE: KEY TERMS, PEOPLE, PLACES, CONCEPTS

- Consumer
- Market equilibrium
- Circular flow
- Hong
- Economic growth

CHAPTER HIGHLIGHTS & NOTES: KEY TERMS, PEOPLE, PLACES, CONCEPTS

Perfect competition	In economic theory, perfect competition describes markets such that no participants are large enough to have the market power to set the price of a homogeneous product. Because the conditions for perfect competition are strict, there are few if any perfectly competitive markets. Still, buyers and sellers in some auction-type markets, say for commodities or some financial assets, may approximate the concept.
Resource	A resource is a source or supply from which benefit is produced. Typically resources are materials, services, staff, or other assets that are transformed to produce benefit and in the process may be consumed or made unavailable. Benefits of resource utilization may include increased wealth, meeting needs or wants, proper functioning of a system, or enhanced well being.
Competitive Market	In economic theory, perfect competition describes markets such that no participants are large enough to have the market power to set the price of a homogeneous product. Because the conditions for perfect competition are strict, there are few if any perfectly competitive markets. Still, buyers and sellers in some auction-type markets, say for commodities (especially decentralised digital commodities such as Bitcoin) or some financial assets, may approximate the concept.
Demand	In economics, demand for a good or service is an entire listing of the quantity of the good or service that a market would choose to buy, for every possible market price of the good or service. (Note: This distinguishes 'demand' from 'quantity demanded', where demand is a listing or graphing of quantity demanded at each possible price. In contrast to demand, quantity demanded is the exact quantity demanded at a certain price.
Law of demand	In economics, the law states that, all else being equal, as the price of a product increases, quantity demanded falls; likewise, as the price of a product decreases, quantity demanded increases.

4. Demand and Supply,

CHAPTER HIGHLIGHTS & NOTES: KEY TERMS, PEOPLE, PLACES, CONCEPTS

	In other words, the law of demand states that the quantity demanded and the price of a commodity are inversely related, other things remaining constant. If the income of the consumer, prices of the related goods, and preferences of the consumer remain unchanged, then the change in quantity of good demanded by the consumer will be negatively correlated to the change in the price of the good.
Demand curve	In economics, the demand curve is the graph depicting the relationship between the price of a certain commodity and the amount of it that consumers are willing and able to purchase at that given price. It is a graphic representation of a demand schedule. The demand curve for all consumers together follows from the demand curve of every individual consumer: the individual demands at each price are added together.
Index	In economics and finance, an index is a statistical measure of changes in a representative group of individual data points. These data may be derived from any number of sources, including company performance, prices, productivity, and employment. Economic indices (index, plural) track economic health from different perspectives.
Market	A market is one of the many varieties of systems, institutions, procedures, social relations and infrastructures whereby parties engage in exchange. While parties may exchange goods and services by barter, most markets rely on sellers offering their goods or services (including labor) in exchange for money from buyers. It can be said that a market is the process by which the prices of goods and services are established.
Import	An import is a good brought into a jurisdiction, especially across a national border, from an external source. The purchaser of the exotic good is called an importer. An import in the receiving country is an export from the sending country.
Price	In ordinary usage, price is the quantity of payment or compensation given by one party to another in return for goods or services. In modern economies, prices are generally expressed in units of some form of currency. (For commodities, they are expressed as currency per unit weight of the commodity, e.g. euros per kilogram).
Inferior good	In economics, an inferior good is a good that decreases in demand when consumer income rises, unlike normal goods, for which the opposite is observed. Normal goods are those for which consumers' demand increases when their income increases. This would be the opposite of a superior good, one that is often associated with wealth and the wealthy, whereas an inferior good is often associated with lower socio-economic groups.

4. Demand and Supply,

CHAPTER HIGHLIGHTS & NOTES: KEY TERMS, PEOPLE, PLACES, CONCEPTS

Normal good	In economics, normal goods are any goods for which demand increases when income increases, and falls when income decreases but price remains constant, i.e. with a positive income elasticity of demand. The term does not necessarily refer to the quality of the good, but an abnormal good would clearly not be in demand, except for possibly lower socioeconomic groups. In particular, when the price of a normal good is zero, the demand is infinite.
Preference	In economics and other social sciences, preference refers to the set of assumptions related to ordering some alternatives, based on the degree of happiness, satisfaction, gratification, enjoyment, or utility they provide, a process which results in an optimal 'choice'. Although economists are usually not interested in choices or preferences in themselves, they are interested in the theory of choice because it serves as a background for empirical demand analysis.
Income	Income is the consumption and savings opportunity gained by an entity within a specified timeframe, which is generally expressed in monetary terms. However, for households and individuals, 'income is the sum of all the wages, salaries, profits, interests payments, rents and other forms of earnings received... in a given period of time.' In the field of public economics, the term may refer to the accumulation of both monetary and non-monetary consumption ability, with the former (monetary) being used as a proxy for total income.
Law of supply	The law of supply is a fundamental principle of economic theory which states that, all else equal, an increase in price results in an increase in quantity supplied. In other words, there is a direct relationship between price and quantity: quantities respond in the same direction as price changes. This means that producers are willing to offer more products for sale on the market at higher prices by increasing production as a way of increasing profits.
Supply	In economics, supply refers to the amount of a product that producers and firms are willing to sell at a given price all other factors being held constant. Usually, supply is plotted as a supply curve showing the relationship of price to the amount of product businesses are willing to sell.
Supply curve	In microeconomics, supply and demand is an economic model of price determination in a market. It concludes that in a competitive market, the unit price for a particular good will vary until it settles at a point where the quantity demanded by consumers (at current price) will equal the quantity supplied by producers (at current price), resulting in an economic equilibrium for price and quantity.

4. Demand and Supply,

CHAPTER HIGHLIGHTS & NOTES: KEY TERMS, PEOPLE, PLACES, CONCEPTS

Product	In marketing, a product is anything that can be offered to a market that might satisfy a want or need. In retailing, products are called merchandise. In manufacturing, products are bought as raw materials and sold as finished goods.
Product differentiation	In economics and marketing, product differentiation is the process of distinguishing a product or service from others, to make it more attractive to a particular target market. This involves differentiating it from competitors' products as well as a firm's own products. The concept was proposed by Edward Chamberlin in his 1933 Theory of Monopolistic Competition.
Price level	The general price level is a hypothetical measure of overall prices for some set of goods and services, in a given region during a given interval, normalized relative to some base set. Typically, a price level is approximated with a price index.
Productivity	Productivity is the ratio of output to inputs in production; it is an average measure of the efficiency of production. Efficiency of production means production's capability to create incomes which is measured by the formula real output value minus real input value. Increasing national productivity can raise living standards because more real income improves people's ability to purchase goods and services, enjoy leisure, improve housing and education and contribute to social and environmental programs.
Consumer	A consumer is a person or group of people, such as a household, who are the final users of products or services. The consumer's use is final in the sense that the product is usually not improved by the use.
Market equilibrium	In economics, economic equilibrium is a state where economic forces such as supply and demand are balanced and in the absence of external influences the values of economic variables will not change. For example, in the standard text-book model of perfect competition, equilibrium occurs at the point at which quantity demanded and quantity supplied are equal. Market equilibrium in this case refers to a condition where a market price is established through competition such that the amount of goods or services sought by buyers is equal to the amount of goods or services produced by sellers.
Circular flow	In economics, the terms circular flow of income or circular flow refer to a simple economic model which describes the reciprocal circulation of income between producers and consumers. In the circular flow model, the inter-dependent entities of producer and consumer are referred to as 'firms' and 'households' respectively and provide each other with factors in order to facilitate the flow of income. Firms provide consumers with goods and services in exchange for consumer expenditure and 'factors of production' from households.
Hong	The Hongs were major business houses in Canton, China and later Hong Kong with significant influence on patterns of consumerism, trade, manufacturing and other key areas of the economy.

4. Demand and Supply,

CHAPTER HIGHLIGHTS & NOTES: KEY TERMS, PEOPLE, PLACES, CONCEPTS

	They were originally led by Howqua as head of the cohong.
Economic growth	Economic growth is the increase in the market value of the goods and services produced by an economy over time. It is conventionally measured as the percent rate of increase in real gross domestic product, or real GDP. Of more importance is the growth of the ratio of GDP to population (GDP per capita), which is also called per capita income. An increase in per capita income is referred to as intensive growth.

CHAPTER QUIZ: KEY TERMS, PEOPLE, PLACES, CONCEPTS

1. In economics, _____s are any goods for which demand increases when income increases, and falls when income decreases but price remains constant, i.e. with a positive income elasticity of demand. The term does not necessarily refer to the quality of the good, but an ab_____ would clearly not be in demand, except for possibly lower socioeconomic groups.

   In particular, when the price of a _____ is zero, the demand is infinite.

   a. Normal good
   b. Cargo
   c. Case
   d. Club good

2. In economics, the _____ is the graph depicting the relationship between the price of a certain commodity and the amount of it that consumers are willing and able to purchase at that given price. It is a graphic representation of a demand schedule. The _____ for all consumers together follows from the _____ of every individual consumer: the individual demands at each price are added together.

   a. Beveridge curve
   b. Demand curve
   c. Contract curve
   d. Cost curve

3. . In economic theory, _____ describes markets such that no participants are large enough to have the market power to set the price of a homogeneous product. Because the conditions for _____ are strict, there are few if any perfectly competitive markets. Still, buyers and sellers in some auction-type markets, say for commodities or some financial assets, may approximate the concept.

   a. Countervailing power
   b. Free entry
   c. Perfect competition

4. Demand and Supply,

CHAPTER QUIZ: KEY TERMS, PEOPLE, PLACES, CONCEPTS

4. In economics, _____ refers to the amount of a product that producers and firms are willing to sell at a given price all other factors being held constant. Usually, _____ is plotted as a _____ curve showing the relationship of price to the amount of product businesses are willing to sell.

   a. Base period
   b. Benefit incidence
   c. Supply
   d. Bond

5. A _____ is a source or supply from which benefit is produced. Typically _____s are materials, services, staff, or other assets that are transformed to produce benefit and in the process may be consumed or made unavailable. Benefits of _____ utilization may include increased wealth, meeting needs or wants, proper functioning of a system, or enhanced well being.

   a. Resource
   b. Gordon-Schaefer Model
   c. Material flow
   d. Material flow accounting

ANSWER KEY
4. Demand and Supply,

1. a
2. b
3. c
4. c
5. a

You can take the complete Online Interactive Chapter Practice Test

for 4. Demand and Supply,
on all key terms, persons, places, and concepts.

No Additional Costs

http://www.Cram101.com

Register, send an email request to Travis.Reese@Cram101.com to get your user Id and password.

Include your customer order number, and ISBN number from your studyguide Retailer.

5. Elasticities of Demand and Supply,

CHAPTER OUTLINE: KEY TERMS, PEOPLE, PLACES, CONCEPTS

_____ Midpoint method _____

_____ Price _____

_____ Price elasticity _____

_____ Demand _____

_____ Elasticity _____

_____ Good _____

_____ Import _____

_____ Demand curve _____

_____ Range _____

_____ Gift _____

_____ Hong _____

_____ Economic growth _____

_____ Income _____

_____ Nature _____

_____ Total revenue _____

_____ Price level _____

_____ Total revenue test _____

_____ Orange _____

_____ Price elasticity of supply _____

_____ Supply _____

_____ Nintendo _____

5. Elasticities of Demand and Supply,

CHAPTER OUTLINE: KEY TERMS, PEOPLE, PLACES, CONCEPTS

	Cross elasticity of demand
	Income elasticity of demand
	Consumer

CHAPTER HIGHLIGHTS & NOTES: KEY TERMS, PEOPLE, PLACES, CONCEPTS

Midpoint method	In numerical analysis, a branch of applied mathematics, the midpoint method is a one-step method for numerically solving the differential equation, $y'(t) = f(t, y(t))$, $y(t_0) = y_0$.

The explicit midpoint method is given by the formula

$$y_{n+1} = y_n + hf\left(t_n + \frac{h}{2}, y_n + \frac{h}{2}f(t_n, y_n)\right), \qquad (1e)$$

the implicit midpoint method by

$$y_{n+1} = y_n + hf\left(t_n + \frac{h}{2}, \frac{1}{2}(y_n + y_{n+1})\right), \qquad (1i)$$

for $n = 0, 1, 2, \ldots$ Here, h is the step size -- a small positive number, $t_n = t_0 + nh$, and y_n is the computed approximate value of $y(t_n)$. The explicit midpoint method is also known as the modified Euler method, the implicit method is the most simple collocation method, and, applied to Hamiltonian dynamics, a symplectic integrator.

The name of the method comes from the fact that in the formula above the function f giving the slope of the solution is evaluated at $t = t_n + h/2$, which is the midpoint between t_n at which the value of y(t) is known and t_{n+1} at which the value of y(t) needs to be found.

The local error at each step of the midpoint method is of order $O(h^3)$, giving a global error of order $O(h^2)$.

5. Elasticities of Demand and Supply,

CHAPTER HIGHLIGHTS & NOTES: KEY TERMS, PEOPLE, PLACES, CONCEPTS

Price	In ordinary usage, price is the quantity of payment or compensation given by one party to another in return for goods or services. In modern economies, prices are generally expressed in units of some form of currency. (For commodities, they are expressed as currency per unit weight of the commodity, e.g. euros per kilogram).
Price elasticity	Price elasticity of demand is a measure used in economics to show the responsiveness, or elasticity, of the quantity demanded of a good or service to a change in its price. More precisely, it gives the percentage change in quantity demanded in response to a one percent change in price (ceteris paribus, i.e. holding constant all the other determinants of demand, such as income). Price elasticities are almost always negative, although analysts tend to ignore the sign even though this can lead to ambiguity.
Demand	In economics, demand for a good or service is an entire listing of the quantity of the good or service that a market would choose to buy, for every possible market price of the good or service. (Note: This distinguishes 'demand' from 'quantity demanded', where demand is a listing or graphing of quantity demanded at each possible price. In contrast to demand, quantity demanded is the exact quantity demanded at a certain price.
Elasticity	In economics, elasticity is the measurement of how responsive an economic variable is to a change in another. For example:•'If I lower the price of my product, how much more will I sell?'•'If I raise the price of one good, how will that affect sales of this other good?'•'If we learn that a resource is becoming scarce, will people scramble to acquire it?' An elastic variable (or elasticity value greater than 1) is one which responds more than proportionally to changes in other variables. In contrast, an inelastic variable (or elasticity value less than 1) is one which changes less than proportionally in response to changes in other variables.
Good	In economics, a good is a material that satisfies human wants and provides utility, for example, to a consumer making a purchase. A common distinction is made between 'goods' that are tangible property (also called goods) and services, which are non-physical. Commodities may be used as a synonym for economic goods but often refer to marketable raw materials and primary products.
Import	An import is a good brought into a jurisdiction, especially across a national border, from an external source. The purchaser of the exotic good is called an importer. An import in the receiving country is an export from the sending country.

5. Elasticities of Demand and Supply,

CHAPTER HIGHLIGHTS & NOTES: KEY TERMS, PEOPLE, PLACES, CONCEPTS

Demand curve	In economics, the demand curve is the graph depicting the relationship between the price of a certain commodity and the amount of it that consumers are willing and able to purchase at that given price. It is a graphic representation of a demand schedule. The demand curve for all consumers together follows from the demand curve of every individual consumer: the individual demands at each price are added together.
Range	In arithmetic, the range of a set of data is the difference between the largest and smallest values. However, in descriptive statistics, this concept of range has a more complex meaning. The range is the size of the smallest interval which contains all the data and provides an indication of statistical dispersion.
Gift	A gift, in the law of property, is the voluntary transfer of property from one person to another (the donee or grantee) without full valuable consideration. In order for a gift to be legally effective, the donor must have intended to give the gift to the donee (donative intent), and the gift must actually be delivered to and accepted by the donee. Gifts can be either:•lifetime gifts (inter vivos gift, donatio inter vivos) - a gift of a present or future interest made and delivered in the donor's lifetime; or•deathbed gifts (gift causa mortis, donatio mortis causa) - a future gift made in expectation of the donor's imminent death.
Hong	The Hongs were major business houses in Canton, China and later Hong Kong with significant influence on patterns of consumerism, trade, manufacturing and other key areas of the economy. They were originally led by Howqua as head of the cohong.
Economic growth	Economic growth is the increase in the market value of the goods and services produced by an economy over time. It is conventionally measured as the percent rate of increase in real gross domestic product, or real GDP. Of more importance is the growth of the ratio of GDP to population (GDP per capita), which is also called per capita income. An increase in per capita income is referred to as intensive growth.
Income	Income is the consumption and savings opportunity gained by an entity within a specified timeframe, which is generally expressed in monetary terms. However, for households and individuals, 'income is the sum of all the wages, salaries, profits, interests payments, rents and other forms of earnings received... in a given period of time.' In the field of public economics, the term may refer to the accumulation of both monetary and non-monetary consumption ability, with the former (monetary) being used as a proxy for total income.

5. Elasticities of Demand and Supply,

CHAPTER HIGHLIGHTS & NOTES: KEY TERMS, PEOPLE, PLACES, CONCEPTS

Nature	Nature is a concept with two major sets of inter-related meanings, referring on the one hand to the things which are natural, or subject to the normal working of 'laws of nature', or on the other hand to the essential properties and causes of those things to be what they naturally are, or in other words the laws of nature themselves. How to understand the meaning and significance of nature has been a consistent theme of discussion within the history of Western Civilization, in the philosophical fields of metaphysics and epistemology, as well as in theology and science. The study of natural things and the regular laws which seem to govern them, as opposed to discussion about what it means to be natural, is the area of natural science.
Total revenue	Total revenue is the total receipts of a firm from the sale of any given quantity of a product. It can be calculated as the selling price of the firm's product times the quantity sold, i.e. total revenue = price × quantity, or letting TR be the total revenue function: $$TR(Q) = P(Q) \times Q$$ where Q is the quantity of output sold, and P(Q) is the inverse demand function (the demand function solved out for price in terms of quantity demanded).
Price level	The general price level is a hypothetical measure of overall prices for some set of goods and services, in a given region during a given interval, normalized relative to some base set. Typically, a price level is approximated with a price index.
Total revenue test	In economics, the Total Revenue Test is a means for determining whether demand is elastic or inelastic. If an increase in price causes an increase in total revenue, then demand can be said to be inelastic, since the increase in price does not have a large impact on quantity demanded. If an increase in price causes a decrease in total revenue, then demand can be said to be elastic, since the increase in price has a large impact on quantity demanded.
Orange	Orange is a component-based data mining and machine learning software suite, featuring a visual programming front-end for explorative data analysis and visualization, and Python bindings and libraries for scripting. It includes a set of components for data preprocessing, feature scoring and filtering, modeling, model evaluation, and exploration techniques. It is implemented in C++ and Python.
Price elasticity of supply	Price elasticity of supply is a measure used in economics to show the responsiveness, or elasticity, of the quantity supplied of a good or service to a change in its price. The elasticity is represented in numerical form, and is defined as the percentage change in the quantity supplied divided by the percentage change in price.

5. Elasticities of Demand and Supply,

CHAPTER HIGHLIGHTS & NOTES: KEY TERMS, PEOPLE, PLACES, CONCEPTS

Supply	In economics, supply refers to the amount of a product that producers and firms are willing to sell at a given price all other factors being held constant. Usually, supply is plotted as a supply curve showing the relationship of price to the amount of product businesses are willing to sell.
Nintendo	Nintendo Co., Ltd. is a Japanese multinational consumer electronics and software company headquartered in Kyoto, Japan. Nintendo is one of the world's largest video game companies by net worth.
Cross elasticity of demand	In economics, the cross elasticity of demand or cross-price elasticity of demand measures the responsiveness of the demand for a good to a change in the price of another good. It is measured as the percentage change in demand for the first good that occurs in response to a percentage change in price of the second good. For example, if, in response to a 10% increase in the price of fuel, the demand of new cars that are fuel inefficient decreased by 20%, the cross elasticity of demand would be: $\frac{-20\%}{10\%} = -2$.
Income elasticity of demand	In economics, income elasticity of demand measures the responsiveness of the demand for a good to a change in the income of the people demanding the good, ceteris paribus. It is calculated as the ratio of the percentage change in demand to the percentage change in income. For example, if, in response to a 10% increase in income, the demand for a good increased by 20%, the income elasticity of demand would be 20%/10% = 2.
Consumer	A consumer is a person or group of people, such as a household, who are the final users of products or services. The consumer's use is final in the sense that the product is usually not improved by the use.

CHAPTER QUIZ: KEY TERMS, PEOPLE, PLACES, CONCEPTS

1. . A _____, in the law of property, is the voluntary transfer of property from one person to another (the donee or grantee) without full valuable consideration. In order for a _____ to be legally effective, the donor must have intended to give the _____ to the donee (donative intent), and the _____ must actually be delivered to and accepted by the donee.

    _____s can be either:•lifetime _____s (inter vivos _____, donatio inter vivos) - a _____ of a present or future interest made and delivered in the donor's lifetime; or•deathbed _____s (_____ causa mortis, donatio mortis causa) - a future _____ made in expectation of the donor's imminent death.

    a. Gift
    b. Beneficial interest
    c. Beneficial owner

5. Elasticities of Demand and Supply,

CHAPTER QUIZ: KEY TERMS, PEOPLE, PLACES, CONCEPTS

2. In numerical analysis, a branch of applied mathematics, the _____ is a one-step method for numerically solving the differential equation, $y'(t) = f(t, y(t)), \quad y(t_0) = y_0$.

    The explicit _____ is given by the formula
    $$y_{n+1} = y_n + hf\left(t_n + \frac{h}{2}, y_n + \frac{h}{2}f(t_n, y_n)\right), \quad (1e)$$

    the implicit _____ by
    $$y_{n+1} = y_n + hf\left(t_n + \frac{h}{2}, \frac{1}{2}(y_n + y_{n+1})\right), \quad (1i)$$

    for $n = 0, 1, 2, \ldots$ Here, h is the step size -- a small positive number, $t_n = t_0 + nh$, and y_n is the computed approximate value of $y(t_n)$. The explicit _____ is also known as the modified Euler method, the implicit method is the most simple collocation method, and, applied to Hamiltionian dynamics, a symplectic integrator.

    The name of the method comes from the fact that in the formula above the function f giving the slope of the solution is evaluated at $t = t_n + h/2$, which is the midpoint between t_n at which the value of y(t) is known and t_{n+1} at which the value of y(t) needs to be found.

    The local error at each step of the _____ is of order $O(h^3)$, giving a global error of order $O(h^2)$.

    a. Midpoint method
    b. Congressional Budget Office choice
    c. Marginal benefit graphical expression
    d. Chiang Mai

3. In arithmetic, the _____ of a set of data is the difference between the largest and smallest values.

    However, in descriptive statistics, this concept of _____ has a more complex meaning. The _____ is the size of the smallest interval which contains all the data and provides an indication of statistical dispersion.

    a. Range
    b. Bhattacharyya distance
    c. Central moment
    d. Coefficient of variation

4. . _____ is a measure used in economics to show the responsiveness, or elasticity, of the quantity supplied of a good or service to a change in its price.

5. Elasticities of Demand and Supply,

CHAPTER QUIZ: KEY TERMS, PEOPLE, PLACES, CONCEPTS

The elasticity is represented in numerical form, and is defined as the percentage change in the quantity supplied divided by the percentage change in price.

When the coefficient is less than one, the said good can be described as inelastic; when the coefficient is greater than one, the supply can be described as elastic.

a. Constant elasticity of substitution
b. Cross elasticity of demand
c. Price elasticity of supply
d. Price elasticity of demand

5. In economics, the _____ or cross-price elasticity of demand measures the responsiveness of the demand for a good to a change in the price of another good. It is measured as the percentage change in demand for the first good that occurs in response to a percentage change in price of the second good. For example, if, in response to a 10% increase in the price of fuel, the demand of new cars that are fuel inefficient decreased by 20%, the _____ would be: $\dfrac{-20\%}{10\%} = -2$.

a. Constant elasticity of substitution
b. Cross elasticity of demand
c. Common Agricultural Policy
d. Commodity Credit Corporation

ANSWER KEY
5. Elasticities of Demand and Supply,

1. a
2. a
3. a
4. c
5. b

You can take the complete Online Interactive Chapter Practice Test

for 5. Elasticities of Demand and Supply,
on all key terms, persons, places, and concepts.

No Additional Costs

http://www.Cram101.com

Register, send an email request to Travis.Reese@Cram101.com to get your user Id and password.

Include your customer order number, and ISBN number from your studyguide Retailer.

6. Efficiency and Fairness of Markets,

CHAPTER OUTLINE: KEY TERMS, PEOPLE, PLACES, CONCEPTS

	Resource
	Price
	Majority rule
	First-come, first-served
	Lottery
	Allocative efficiency
	Industrial Revolution
	Product differentiation
	Production
	Production possibilities frontier
	Circular flow
	Efficiency
	Resource allocation
	Marginal cost
	Demand
	Demand curve
	Consumer
	Consumer surplus
	Cost
	Supply
	Market

6. Efficiency and Fairness of Markets,

CHAPTER OUTLINE: KEY TERMS, PEOPLE, PLACES, CONCEPTS

	Invisible hand
	Perfect competition
	Wealth
	Wealth of Nations
	Competitive Market
	E-commerce
	Rate
	Deadweight loss
	Market failure
	Overproduction
	Income
	Public good
	Subsidies
	Taxes
	Profit
	Cost-push inflation
	Transaction cost
	Factor
	Index
	Price gouging
	Compromise

6. Efficiency and Fairness of Markets,

CHAPTER HIGHLIGHTS & NOTES: KEY TERMS, PEOPLE, PLACES, CONCEPTS

Resource	A resource is a source or supply from which benefit is produced. Typically resources are materials, services, staff, or other assets that are transformed to produce benefit and in the process may be consumed or made unavailable. Benefits of resource utilization may include increased wealth, meeting needs or wants, proper functioning of a system, or enhanced well being.
Price	In ordinary usage, price is the quantity of payment or compensation given by one party to another in return for goods or services. In modern economies, prices are generally expressed in units of some form of currency. (For commodities, they are expressed as currency per unit weight of the commodity, e.g. euros per kilogram).
Majority rule	Majority rule is a decision rule that selects alternatives which have a majority, that is, more than half the votes. It is the binary decision rule used most often in influential decision-making bodies, including the legislatures of democratic nations. Distinction with plurality Though plurality (first-past-the post) is often mistaken for majority rule, they are not the same.
First-come, first-served	First-come, first-served - sometimes first-in, first-served and first-come, first choice - is a service policy whereby the requests of customers or clients are attended to in the order that they arrived, without other biases or preferences. The policy can be employed when processing sales orders, in determining restaurant seating, on a taxi stand, etc. In Western society, it is the standard policy for the processing of most queues in which people wait for a service.
Lottery	In expected utility theory, a lottery is a discrete distribution of probability on a set of states of nature. The elements of a lottery correspond to the probability that a certain outcome arises from a given state of nature. In economics, individuals are assumed to rank lotteries according to a rational system of preferences, although it is now accepted that people make irrational choices systematically.
Allocative efficiency	Allocative efficiency is a type of economic efficiency in which economy/producers produce only those types of goods and services that are more desirable in the society and also in high demand. According to the formula the point of allocative efficiency is a point where price is equal to marginal cost (P=MC) or (MC=MR). At this point the social surplus is maximized with no deadweight loss, or the value society puts on that level of output produced minus the value of resources used to achieve that level, yet can be applied to other things such as level of pollution.
Industrial Revolution	The Industrial Revolution was the transition to new manufacturing processes in the period from about 1760 to sometime between 1820 and 1840.

6. Efficiency and Fairness of Markets,

CHAPTER HIGHLIGHTS & NOTES: KEY TERMS, PEOPLE, PLACES, CONCEPTS

	This transition included going from hand production methods to machines, new chemical manufacturing and iron production processes, improved efficiency of water power, the increasing use of steam power and the development of machine tools. It also included the change from wood and other bio-fuels to coal.
	Textiles were the dominant industry of the Industrial Revolution in terms of employment, value of output and capital invested.
Product differentiation	In economics and marketing, product differentiation is the process of distinguishing a product or service from others, to make it more attractive to a particular target market. This involves differentiating it from competitors' products as well as a firm's own products. The concept was proposed by Edward Chamberlin in his 1933 Theory of Monopolistic Competition.
Production	Production is a process of combining various material inputs and immaterial inputs in order to make something for consumption (the output). It is the act of creating output, a good or service which has value and contributes to the utility of individuals. Economic well-being is created in a production process, meaning all economic activities that aim directly or indirectly to satisfy human needs.
Production possibilities frontier	In economics, a production-possibility frontier, sometimes called a production-possibility curve, production-possibility boundary or product transformation curve, is a graph that shows the various combinations of amounts that two commodities could produce using the same fixed total amount of each of the factors of production. Graphically bounding the production set for fixed input quantities, the production possibilities frontier curve shows the maximum possible production level of one commodity for any given production level of the other, given the existing state of technology. By doing so, it defines productive efficiency in the context of that production set: a point on the frontier indicates efficient use of the available inputs, while a point beneath the curve indicates inefficiency.
Circular flow	In economics, the terms circular flow of income or circular flow refer to a simple economic model which describes the reciprocal circulation of income between producers and consumers. In the circular flow model, the inter-dependent entities of producer and consumer are referred to as 'firms' and 'households' respectively and provide each other with factors in order to facilitate the flow of income. Firms provide consumers with goods and services in exchange for consumer expenditure and 'factors of production' from households.
Efficiency	The relative efficiency of two procedures is the ratio of their efficiencies, although often this term is used where the comparison is made between a given procedure and a notional 'best possible' procedure. The efficiencies and the relative efficiency of two procedures theoretically depend on the sample size available for the given procedure, but it is often possible to use the asymptotic relative efficiency as the principal comparison measure.

6. Efficiency and Fairness of Markets,

CHAPTER HIGHLIGHTS & NOTES: KEY TERMS, PEOPLE, PLACES, CONCEPTS

Resource allocation	Resource allocation is used to assign the available resources in an economic way. It is part of resource management. In project management, resource allocation is the scheduling of activities and the resources required by those activities while taking into consideration both the resource availability and the project time.
Marginal cost	In economics and finance, marginal cost is the change in the total cost that arises when the quantity produced has an increment by unit. That is, it is the cost of producing one more unit of a good. In general terms, marginal cost at each level of production includes any additional costs required to produce the next unit.
Demand	In economics, demand for a good or service is an entire listing of the quantity of the good or service that a market would choose to buy, for every possible market price of the good or service. (Note: This distinguishes 'demand' from 'quantity demanded', where demand is a listing or graphing of quantity demanded at each possible price. In contrast to demand, quantity demanded is the exact quantity demanded at a certain price.
Demand curve	In economics, the demand curve is the graph depicting the relationship between the price of a certain commodity and the amount of it that consumers are willing and able to purchase at that given price. It is a graphic representation of a demand schedule. The demand curve for all consumers together follows from the demand curve of every individual consumer: the individual demands at each price are added together.
Consumer	A consumer is a person or group of people, such as a household, who are the final users of products or services. The consumer's use is final in the sense that the product is usually not improved by the use.
Consumer surplus	In mainstream economics, economic surplus (also known as total welfare or Marshallian surplus) refers to two related quantities. Consumer surplus or consumers' surplus is the monetary gain obtained by consumers because they are able to purchase a product for a price that is less than the highest price that they would be willing to pay. Producer surplus or producers' surplus is the amount that producers benefit by selling at a market price that is higher than the least that they would be willing to sell for.
Cost	In production, research, retail, and accounting, a cost is the value of money that has been used up to produce something, and hence is not available for use anymore. In business, the cost may be one of acquisition, in which case the amount of money expended to acquire it is counted as cost. In this case, money is the input that is gone in order to acquire the thing.
Supply	In economics, supply refers to the amount of a product that producers and firms are willing to sell at a given price all other factors being held constant. Usually, supply is plotted as a supply curve showing the relationship of price to the amount of product businesses are willing to sell.

6. Efficiency and Fairness of Markets,

CHAPTER HIGHLIGHTS & NOTES: KEY TERMS, PEOPLE, PLACES, CONCEPTS

Market	A market is one of the many varieties of systems, institutions, procedures, social relations and infrastructures whereby parties engage in exchange. While parties may exchange goods and services by barter, most markets rely on sellers offering their goods or services (including labor) in exchange for money from buyers. It can be said that a market is the process by which the prices of goods and services are established.
Invisible hand	In economics, the invisible hand of the market is a metaphor conceived by Adam Smith to describe the self-regulating behavior of the marketplace. Individuals can make profit, and maximize it without the need for government intervention. The exact phrase is used just three times in Smith's writings, but has come to capture his important claim that individuals' efforts to maximize their own gains in a free market may benefit society, even if the ambitious have no benevolent intentions.
Perfect competition	In economic theory, perfect competition describes markets such that no participants are large enough to have the market power to set the price of a homogeneous product. Because the conditions for perfect competition are strict, there are few if any perfectly competitive markets. Still, buyers and sellers in some auction-type markets, say for commodities or some financial assets, may approximate the concept.
Wealth	The modern understanding of Wealth is the abundance of valuable resources or material possessions. This excludes the core meaning as held in the originating old English word weal, which is from an Indo-European word stem. In this larger understanding of wealth, an individual, community, region or country that possesses an abundance of such possessions or resources to the benefit of the common good is known as wealthy.
Wealth of Nations	An Inquiry into the Nature and Causes of the Wealth of Nations, generally referred to by its shortened title The Wealth of Nations, is the magnum opus of the Scottish economist and moral philosopher Adam Smith. First published in 1776, the book offers one of the world's first collected descriptions of what builds nations' wealth and is today a fundamental work in classical economics. Through reflection over the economics at the beginning of the Industrial Revolution the book touches upon such broad topics as the division of labour, productivity and free markets.
Competitive Market	In economic theory, perfect competition describes markets such that no participants are large enough to have the market power to set the price of a homogeneous product. Because the conditions for perfect competition are strict, there are few if any perfectly competitive markets. Still, buyers and sellers in some auction-type markets, say for commodities (especially decentralised digital commodities such as Bitcoin) or some financial assets, may approximate the concept.
E-commerce	Electronic commerce, commonly known as E-commerce or eCommerce, is a type of industry where the buying and selling of products or services is conducted over electronic systems such as the Internet and other computer networks.

6. Efficiency and Fairness of Markets,

CHAPTER HIGHLIGHTS & NOTES: KEY TERMS, PEOPLE, PLACES, CONCEPTS

	Electronic commerce draws on technologies such as mobile commerce, electronic funds transfer, supply chain management, Internet marketing, online transaction processing, electronic data interchange (EDI), inventory management systems, and automated data collection systems. Modern electronic commerce typically uses the World Wide Web at least at one point in the transaction's life-cycle, although it may encompass a wider range of technologies such as e-mail, mobile devices, social media, and telephones as well.
Rate	In mathematics, a rate is a ratio between two measurements with different units. If the unit or quantity in respect of which something is changing is not specified, usually the rate is per unit time. However, a rate of change can be specified per unit time, or per unit of length or mass or another quantity.
Deadweight loss	In economics, a deadweight loss is a loss of economic efficiency that can occur when equilibrium for a good or service is not Pareto optimal. Causes of deadweight loss can include monopoly pricing (in the case of artificial scarcity), externalities, taxes or subsidies, and binding price ceilings or floors (including minimum wages). The term deadweight loss may also be referred to as the 'excess burden' of monopoly or taxation.
Market failure	Market failure is a concept within economic theory describing when the allocation of goods and services by a free market is not efficient. That is, there exists another conceivable outcome where a market participant may be made better-off without making someone else worse-off. (The outcome is not Pareto optimal).
Overproduction	In economics, overproduction, oversupply or excess of supply refers to excess of supply over demand of products being offered to the market. This leads to lower prices and/or unsold goods along with the possibility of unemployment. The demand side equivalent is underconsumption; some consider supply and demand two sides to the same coin - excess supply is only relative to a given demand, and insufficient demand is only relative to a given supply - and thus consider overproduction and underconsumption equivalent.
Income	Income is the consumption and savings opportunity gained by an entity within a specified timeframe, which is generally expressed in monetary terms. However, for households and individuals, 'income is the sum of all the wages, salaries, profits, interests payments, rents and other forms of earnings received... in a given period of time.' In the field of public economics, the term may refer to the accumulation of both monetary and non-monetary consumption ability, with the former (monetary) being used as a proxy for total income.

6. Efficiency and Fairness of Markets,

CHAPTER HIGHLIGHTS & NOTES: KEY TERMS, PEOPLE, PLACES, CONCEPTS

Public good	In economics, a public good is a good that is both non-excludable and non-rivalrous in that individuals cannot be effectively excluded from use and where use by one individual does not reduce availability to others. Examples of public goods include fresh air, knowledge, lighthouses, national defense, flood control systems and street lighting. Public goods that are available everywhere are sometimes referred to as global public goods.
Subsidies	A subsidy is a form of financial or in kind support extended to an economic sector generally with the aim of promoting economic and social policy. Although commonly extended from Government, the term subsidy can relate to any type of support - for example from NGOs or implicit subsidies. Subsidies come in various forms including: direct (cash grants, interest-free loans) and indirect (tax breaks, insurance, low-interest loans, depreciation write-offs, rent rebates).
Taxes	A tax is a financial charge or other levy imposed upon a taxpayer (an individual or legal entity) by a state or the functional equivalent of a state such that failure to pay is punishable by law. Taxes are also imposed by many administrative divisions. Taxes consist of direct or indirect taxes and may be paid in money or as its labour equivalent.
Profit	In neoclassical microeconomic theory, the term profit has two related but distinct meanings. Economic profit is similar to accounting profit but smaller because it reflects the total opportunity costs (both explicit and implicit) of a venture to an investor. Normal profit refers to a situation in which the economic profit is zero.
Cost-push inflation	Cost-push inflation is an alleged type of inflation caused by substantial increases in the cost of important goods or services where no suitable alternative is available. A situation that has been often cited of this was the oil crisis of the 1970s, which some economists see as a major cause of the inflation experienced in the Western world in that decade. It is argued that this inflation resulted from increases in the cost of petroleum imposed by the member states of OPEC. Since petroleum is so important to industrialised economies, a large increase in its price can lead to the increase in the price of most products, raising the inflation rate.
Transaction cost	In economics and related disciplines, a transaction cost is a cost incurred in making an economic exchange . Transaction costs can be divided into three broad categories:•Search and information costs are costs such as those incurred in determining that the required good is available on the market, which has the lowest price, etc.•Bargaining costs are the costs required to come to an acceptable agreement with the other party to the transaction, drawing up an appropriate contract and so on. In game theory this is analyzed for instance in the game of chicken.
Factor	A factor, Latin for 'doer, maker', is a mercantile fiduciary who receives and sells goods on commission (called factorage), transacting business in his own name and not disclosing his principal, and historically with his seat at a factory (trading post).

6. Efficiency and Fairness of Markets,

CHAPTER HIGHLIGHTS & NOTES: KEY TERMS, PEOPLE, PLACES, CONCEPTS

	A factor differs from a commission merchant in that a factor takes possession of goods (or documents of title representing goods) on consignment, whereas a commission merchant sells goods not in his possession on the basis of samples. Most modern factor business is in the textile field, but factors are also used to a great extent in the shoe, furniture, hardware, and other industries, and the trade areas in which factors operate have increased.
Index	In economics and finance, an index is a statistical measure of changes in a representative group of individual data points. These data may be derived from any number of sources, including company performance, prices, productivity, and employment. Economic indices (index, plural) track economic health from different perspectives.
Price gouging	Price gouging is a pejorative term referring to a situation in which a seller prices goods or commodities at a level much higher than is considered reasonable or fair. This rapid increase in prices occurs after a demand or supply shock: examples include price increases after hurricanes or other natural disasters. In precise, legal usage, it is the name of a crime that applies in some of the United States during civil emergencies.
Compromise	To compromise is to make a deal between different parties where each party gives up part of their demand. In arguments, compromise is a concept of finding agreement through communication, through a mutual acceptance of terms--often involving variations from an original goal or desire. Extremism is often considered as antonym to compromise, which, depending on context, may be associated with concepts of balance and tolerance.

CHAPTER QUIZ: KEY TERMS, PEOPLE, PLACES, CONCEPTS

1. _____ is a concept within economic theory describing when the allocation of goods and services by a free market is not efficient. That is, there exists another conceivable outcome where a market participant may be made better-off without making someone else worse-off. (The outcome is not Pareto optimal).

    a. Market failure
    b. Bankruptcy
    c. Benefit shortfall
    d. Climate change

2. . A _____ is a source or supply from which benefit is produced. Typically _____s are materials, services, staff, or other assets that are transformed to produce benefit and in the process may be consumed or made unavailable. Benefits of _____ utilization may include increased wealth, meeting needs or wants, proper functioning of a system, or enhanced well being.

6. Efficiency and Fairness of Markets,

CHAPTER QUIZ: KEY TERMS, PEOPLE, PLACES, CONCEPTS

   a. Crude
   b. Gordon-Schaefer Model
   c. Resource
   d. Material flow accounting

3. In economic theory, perfect competition describes markets such that no participants are large enough to have the market power to set the price of a homogeneous product. Because the conditions for perfect competition are strict, there are few if any perfectly _____s. Still, buyers and sellers in some auction-type markets, say for commodities (especially decentralised digital commodities such as Bitcoin) or some financial assets, may approximate the concept.

   a. Pure competition
   b. Competitive Market
   c. Congressional Budget Office choice
   d. Bankruptcy tourism

4. In ordinary usage, _____ is the quantity of payment or compensation given by one party to another in return for goods or services.

   In modern economies, _____s are generally expressed in units of some form of currency. (For commodities, they are expressed as currency per unit weight of the commodity, e.g. euros per kilogram).

   a. Back to school
   b. Backward invention
   c. Price
   d. Bayesian inference in marketing

5. _____ - sometimes first-in, first-served and first-come, first choice - is a service policy whereby the requests of customers or clients are attended to in the order that they arrived, without other biases or preferences. The policy can be employed when processing sales orders, in determining restaurant seating, on a taxi stand, etc. In Western society, it is the standard policy for the processing of most queues in which people wait for a service.

   a. 2007 Gasoline Rationing Plan in Iran
   b. Bratt System
   c. CC41
   d. First-come, first-served

ANSWER KEY
6. Efficiency and Fairness of Markets,

1. a
2. c
3. b
4. c
5. d

You can take the complete Online Interactive Chapter Practice Test

for 6. Efficiency and Fairness of Markets,
on all key terms, persons, places, and concepts.

No Additional Costs

http://www.Cram101.com

Register, send an email request to Travis.Reese@Cram101.com to get your user Id and password.

Include your customer order number, and ISBN number from your studyguide Retailer.

7. Government Actions in Markets,

CHAPTER OUTLINE: KEY TERMS, PEOPLE, PLACES, CONCEPTS

_____ Market

_____ Market equilibrium

_____ Tax incidence

_____ Incidence

_____ Deadweight loss

_____ Circular flow

_____ Efficiency

_____ Taxes

_____ Excess burden

_____ Industrial Revolution

_____ Elasticity

_____ Inefficiency

_____ Demand

_____ Elasticity of demand

_____ Supply

_____ Price ceiling

_____ Price

_____ Black market

_____ Factor

_____ Production

_____ Labor force

7. Government Actions in Markets,

CHAPTER OUTLINE: KEY TERMS, PEOPLE, PLACES, CONCEPTS

	Price floor
	Value
	Minimum wage
	Minimum wage law
	Law
	Unemployment
	Executive officer
	Labor union
	Price support
	Product support
	Domestic market

CHAPTER HIGHLIGHTS & NOTES: KEY TERMS, PEOPLE, PLACES, CONCEPTS

Market	A market is one of the many varieties of systems, institutions, procedures, social relations and infrastructures whereby parties engage in exchange. While parties may exchange goods and services by barter, most markets rely on sellers offering their goods or services (including labor) in exchange for money from buyers. It can be said that a market is the process by which the prices of goods and services are established.
Market equilibrium	In economics, economic equilibrium is a state where economic forces such as supply and demand are balanced and in the absence of external influences the values of economic variables will not change. For example, in the standard text-book model of perfect competition, equilibrium occurs at the point at which quantity demanded and quantity supplied are equal.

7. Government Actions in Markets,

CHAPTER HIGHLIGHTS & NOTES: KEY TERMS, PEOPLE, PLACES, CONCEPTS

Tax incidence	In economics, tax incidence is the analysis of the effect of a particular tax on the distribution of economic welfare. Tax incidence is said to 'fall' upon the group that ultimately bears the burden of, or ultimately has to pay, the tax. The key concept is that the tax incidence or tax burden does not depend on where the revenue is collected, but on the price elasticity of demand and price elasticity of supply.
Incidence	Incidence is a measure of the risk of developing some new condition within a specified period of time. Although sometimes loosely expressed simply as the number of new cases during some time period, it is better expressed as a proportion or a rate with a denominator. Incidence proportion (also known as cumulative incidence) is the number of new cases within a specified time period divided by the size of the population initially at risk.
Deadweight loss	In economics, a deadweight loss is a loss of economic efficiency that can occur when equilibrium for a good or service is not Pareto optimal. Causes of deadweight loss can include monopoly pricing (in the case of artificial scarcity), externalities, taxes or subsidies, and binding price ceilings or floors (including minimum wages). The term deadweight loss may also be referred to as the 'excess burden' of monopoly or taxation.
Circular flow	In economics, the terms circular flow of income or circular flow refer to a simple economic model which describes the reciprocal circulation of income between producers and consumers. In the circular flow model, the inter-dependent entities of producer and consumer are referred to as 'firms' and 'households' respectively and provide each other with factors in order to facilitate the flow of income. Firms provide consumers with goods and services in exchange for consumer expenditure and 'factors of production' from households.
Efficiency	The relative efficiency of two procedures is the ratio of their efficiencies, although often this term is used where the comparison is made between a given procedure and a notional 'best possible' procedure. The efficiencies and the relative efficiency of two procedures theoretically depend on the sample size available for the given procedure, but it is often possible to use the asymptotic relative efficiency as the principal comparison measure. Efficiencies are often defined using the variance or mean square error as the measure of desirability.
Taxes	A tax is a financial charge or other levy imposed upon a taxpayer (an individual or legal entity) by a state or the functional equivalent of a state such that failure to pay is punishable by law. Taxes are also imposed by many administrative divisions. Taxes consist of direct or indirect taxes and may be paid in money or as its labour equivalent.

7. Government Actions in Markets,

CHAPTER HIGHLIGHTS & NOTES: KEY TERMS, PEOPLE, PLACES, CONCEPTS

Excess burden	In economics, a deadweight loss (also known as excess burden or allocative inefficiency) is a loss of economic efficiency that can occur when equilibrium for a good or service is not Pareto optimal. Causes of deadweight loss can include monopoly pricing, externalities, taxes or subsidies, and binding price ceilings or floors (including minimum wages). The term deadweight loss may also be referred to as the 'excess burden' of monopoly or taxation.
Industrial Revolution	The Industrial Revolution was the transition to new manufacturing processes in the period from about 1760 to sometime between 1820 and 1840. This transition included going from hand production methods to machines, new chemical manufacturing and iron production processes, improved efficiency of water power, the increasing use of steam power and the development of machine tools. It also included the change from wood and other bio-fuels to coal. Textiles were the dominant industry of the Industrial Revolution in terms of employment, value of output and capital invested.
Elasticity	In economics, elasticity is the measurement of how responsive an economic variable is to a change in another. For example:•'If I lower the price of my product, how much more will I sell?'•'If I raise the price of one good, how will that affect sales of this other good?'•'If we learn that a resource is becoming scarce, will people scramble to acquire it?' An elastic variable (or elasticity value greater than 1) is one which responds more than proportionally to changes in other variables. In contrast, an inelastic variable (or elasticity value less than 1) is one which changes less than proportionally in response to changes in other variables.
Inefficiency	The term inefficiency has several meanings depending on the context in which its used:•Distributive Inefficiency - refers to the inefficient distribution of income and wealth within a society. Decreasing marginal utilities of wealth suggests that more egalitarian distributions of wealth are more efficient than unegalitarian distributions. Distributive inefficiency is often associated with economic inequality.•Economic inefficiency - refers to a situation where 'we could be doing a better job,' i.e., attaining our goals at lower cost.
Demand	In economics, demand for a good or service is an entire listing of the quantity of the good or service that a market would choose to buy, for every possible market price of the good or service. (Note: This distinguishes 'demand' from 'quantity demanded', where demand is a listing or graphing of quantity demanded at each possible price. In contrast to demand, quantity demanded is the exact quantity demanded at a certain price.
Elasticity of demand	Price elasticity of demand is a measure used in economics to show the responsiveness, or elasticity, of the quantity demanded of a good or service to a change in its price.

7. Government Actions in Markets,

CHAPTER HIGHLIGHTS & NOTES: KEY TERMS, PEOPLE, PLACES, CONCEPTS

	More precisely, it gives the percentage change in quantity demanded in response to a one percent change in price (ceteris paribus, i.e. holding constant all the other determinants of demand, such as income).
	Price elasticities are almost always negative, although analysts tend to ignore the sign even though this can lead to ambiguity.
Supply	In economics, supply refers to the amount of a product that producers and firms are willing to sell at a given price all other factors being held constant. Usually, supply is plotted as a supply curve showing the relationship of price to the amount of product businesses are willing to sell.
Price ceiling	A price ceiling is a government-imposed price control or limit on how high a price is charged for a product. Governments intend price ceilings to protect consumers from conditions that could make necessary commodities unattainable. However, a price ceiling can cause problems if imposed for a long period without controlled rationing.
Price	In ordinary usage, price is the quantity of payment or compensation given by one party to another in return for goods or services.
	In modern economies, prices are generally expressed in units of some form of currency. (For commodities, they are expressed as currency per unit weight of the commodity, e.g. euros per kilogram).
Black market	A black market or underground economy is the market in which goods or services are traded illegally. The key distinction of a black market trade is that the transaction itself is illegal. The goods or services may or may not themselves be illegal to own, or to trade through other, legal channels.
Factor	A factor, Latin for 'doer, maker', is a mercantile fiduciary who receives and sells goods on commission (called factorage), transacting business in his own name and not disclosing his principal, and historically with his seat at a factory (trading post). A factor differs from a commission merchant in that a factor takes possession of goods (or documents of title representing goods) on consignment, whereas a commission merchant sells goods not in his possession on the basis of samples. Most modern factor business is in the textile field, but factors are also used to a great extent in the shoe, furniture, hardware, and other industries, and the trade areas in which factors operate have increased.
Production	Production is a process of combining various material inputs and immaterial inputs in order to make something for consumption (the output). It is the act of creating output, a good or service which has value and contributes to the utility of individuals. Economic well-being is created in a production process, meaning all economic activities that aim directly or indirectly to satisfy human needs.
Labor force	The labor force is the actual number of people available for work.

7. Government Actions in Markets,

CHAPTER HIGHLIGHTS & NOTES: KEY TERMS, PEOPLE, PLACES, CONCEPTS

	The labor force of a country includes both the employed and the unemployed. The labor force participation rate, LFPR (or economic activity rate, EAR), is the ratio between the labor force and the overall size of their cohort (national population of the same age range).
Price floor	A price floor is a government- or group-imposed price control or limit on how low a price can be charged for a product. A price floor must be greater than the equilibrium price in order to be effective.
Value	Economic value is a measure of the benefit that an economic actor can gain from either a good or service. It is generally measured relative to units of currency, and the interpretation is therefore 'what is the maximum amount of money a specific actor is willing and able to pay for the good or service'? Note that economic value is not the same as market price. If a consumer is willing to buy a good, it implies that the customer places a higher value on the good than the market price.
Minimum wage	A minimum wage is the lowest hourly, daily or monthly remuneration that employers may legally pay to workers. Equivalently, it is the lowest wage at which workers may sell their labor. Although minimum wage laws are in effect in many jurisdictions, differences of opinion exist about the benefits and drawbacks of a minimum wage.
Minimum wage law	Minimum wage law is the body of law which prohibits employers from hiring employees or workers for less than a given hourly, daily or monthly minimum wage. More than 90% of all countries have some kind of minimum wage legislation. Until recently, minimum wage laws were usually very tightly focused.
Law	In mathematics, the law of a stochastic process is the measure that the process induces on the collection of functions from the index set into the state space. The law encodes a lot of information about the process; in the case of a random walk, for example, the law is the probability distribution of the possible trajectories of the walk.
Unemployment	Unemployment occurs when people are without work and actively seeking work. The unemployment rate is a measure of the prevalence of unemployment and it is calculated as a percentage by dividing the number of unemployed individuals by all individuals currently in the labor force. During periods of recession, an economy usually experiences a relatively high unemployment rate.
Executive officer	An executive officer is generally a person responsible for running an organization, although the exact nature of the role varies depending on the organization.

7. Government Actions in Markets,

CHAPTER HIGHLIGHTS & NOTES: KEY TERMS, PEOPLE, PLACES, CONCEPTS

Labor union	A trade union, labour union (Canadian English), or labor union is an organization of workers who have come together to achieve common goals such as protecting the integrity of its trade, improving safety standards, achieving higher pay and benefits such as health care and retirement, increasing the number of employees an employer assigns to complete the work, and better working conditions. The trade union, through its leadership, bargains with the employer on behalf of union members (rank and file members) and negotiates labour contracts (collective bargaining) with employers. The most common purpose of these associations or unions is 'maintaining or improving the conditions of their employment'.
Price support	In economics, a price support may be either a subsidy or a price control, both with the intended effect of keeping the market price of a good higher than the competitive equilibrium level.
	In the case of a price control, a price support is the minimum legal price a seller may charge, typically placed above equilibrium. It is the support of certain price levels at or above market values by the government.
Product support	Product support is a service provided by many retailers of various products, primarily electronics, that provides the end-user with a resource for information regarding the product, and help if the product should malfunction. Product Support can be found in most manuals for products in the form of a phone number, website address, or physical location.
	The Internet has allowed for a new form of product support to develop.
Domestic market	A domestic market is a financial market. Its trades are aimed toward a single market. A domestic market is also referred to as domestic trading.

CHAPTER QUIZ: KEY TERMS, PEOPLE, PLACES, CONCEPTS

1. . The _____ was the transition to new manufacturing processes in the period from about 1760 to sometime between 1820 and 1840. This transition included going from hand production methods to machines, new chemical manufacturing and iron production processes, improved efficiency of water power, the increasing use of steam power and the development of machine tools. It also included the change from wood and other bio-fuels to coal.

   Textiles were the dominant industry of the _____ in terms of employment, value of output and capital invested.

   a. Bendigo Petition
   b. Bacon
   c. Industrial Revolution

7. Government Actions in Markets,

CHAPTER QUIZ: KEY TERMS, PEOPLE, PLACES, CONCEPTS

2. In economics, a _____ is a loss of economic efficiency that can occur when equilibrium for a good or service is not Pareto optimal.

   Causes of _____ can include monopoly pricing (in the case of artificial scarcity), externalities, taxes or subsidies, and binding price ceilings or floors (including minimum wages). The term _____ may also be referred to as the 'excess burden' of monopoly or taxation.

   a. Scarcity
   b. Deadweight loss
   c. Grain supply to the city of Rome
   d. Household plot

3. A _____ is a government-imposed price control or limit on how high a price is charged for a product. Governments intend _____s to protect consumers from conditions that could make necessary commodities unattainable. However, a _____ can cause problems if imposed for a long period without controlled rationing.

   a. Price ceiling
   b. National Mobilization Law
   c. Price support
   d. Socialist accumulation

4. A _____ is one of the many varieties of systems, institutions, procedures, social relations and infrastructures whereby parties engage in exchange. While parties may exchange goods and services by barter, most _____s rely on sellers offering their goods or services (including labor) in exchange for money from buyers. It can be said that a _____ is the process by which the prices of goods and services are established.

   a. Contract farming
   b. Convertible husbandry
   c. Corn exchange
   d. Market

5. A tax is a financial charge or other levy imposed upon a taxpayer (an individual or legal entity) by a state or the functional equivalent of a state such that failure to pay is punishable by law. _____ are also imposed by many administrative divisions. _____ consist of direct or indirect _____ and may be paid in money or as its labour equivalent.

   a. Marginal cost of public funds
   b. Public Expenditure Statistical Analyses
   c. Ways and means advances
   d. Taxes

ANSWER KEY
7. Government Actions in Markets,

1. c
2. b
3. a
4. d
5. d

You can take the complete Online Interactive Chapter Practice Test

for 7. Government Actions in Markets,
on all key terms, persons, places, and concepts.

No Additional Costs

http://www.Cram101.com

Register, send an email request to Travis.Reese@Cram101.com to get your user Id and password.

Include your customer order number, and ISBN number from your studyguide Retailer.

8. Global Markets in Action,

CHAPTER OUTLINE: KEY TERMS, PEOPLE, PLACES, CONCEPTS

- _____ Comparative advantage
- _____ Export
- _____ Import
- _____ International trade
- _____ National
- _____ Outsourcing
- _____ Trade
- _____ Rate
- _____ Market
- _____ Globalization
- _____ Producer surplus
- _____ General Agreement on Tariffs and Trade
- _____ Tariff
- _____ World Trade Organization
- _____ Product differentiation
- _____ Consumer
- _____ Deadweight loss
- _____ Import quota
- _____ Subsidies
- _____ Voluntary export restraints
- _____ Export subsidy

8. Global Markets in Action,

CHAPTER OUTLINE: KEY TERMS, PEOPLE, PLACES, CONCEPTS

	Protection
	Dumping
	Diversity
	Stability

CHAPTER HIGHLIGHTS & NOTES: KEY TERMS, PEOPLE, PLACES, CONCEPTS

Comparative advantage	In economics, comparative advantage refers to the ability of a party to produce a particular good or service at a lower marginal and opportunity cost over another. Even if one country is more efficient in the production of all goods (absolute advantage in all goods) than the other, both countries will still gain by trading with each other, as long as they have different relative efficiencies. For example, if, using machinery, a worker in one country can produce both shoes and shirts at 6 per hour, and a worker in a country with less machinery can produce either 2 shoes or 4 shirts in an hour, each country can gain from trade because their internal trade-offs between shoes and shirts are different.
Export	The term export means shipping the goods and services out of the port of a country. The seller of such goods and services is referred to as an 'exporter' who is based in the country of export whereas the overseas based buyer is referred to as an 'importer'. In International Trade, 'exports' refers to selling goods and services produced in the home country to other markets.
Import	An import is a good brought into a jurisdiction, especially across a national border, from an external source. The purchaser of the exotic good is called an importer. An import in the receiving country is an export from the sending country.
International trade	International trade is the exchange of capital, goods, and services across international borders or territories. In most countries, such trade represents a significant share of gross domestic product (GDP). While international trade has been present throughout much of history, its economic, social, and political importance has been on the rise in recent centuries.
National	National is an adjective (adverb form: nationally) used to describe a product or publication that is distributed throughout an entire nation, e.g., a national magazine. It implies that the item is available for purchase or access anywhere in the country.

8. Global Markets in Action,

CHAPTER HIGHLIGHTS & NOTES: KEY TERMS, PEOPLE, PLACES, CONCEPTS

Outsourcing	In business, outsourcing is the contracting out of a business process to a third-party. The term 'outsourcing' became popular in the United States near the turn of the 21st century. Outsourcing sometimes involves transferring employees and assets from one firm to another, but not always.
Trade	Trade, also called goods exchange economy, is to transfer the ownership of goods from one person or entity to another by getting a product or service in exchange from the buyer. Trade is sometimes loosely called commerce or financial transaction or barter. A network that allows trade is called a market.
Rate	In mathematics, a rate is a ratio between two measurements with different units. If the unit or quantity in respect of which something is changing is not specified, usually the rate is per unit time. However, a rate of change can be specified per unit time, or per unit of length or mass or another quantity.
Market	A market is one of the many varieties of systems, institutions, procedures, social relations and infrastructures whereby parties engage in exchange. While parties may exchange goods and services by barter, most markets rely on sellers offering their goods or services (including labor) in exchange for money from buyers. It can be said that a market is the process by which the prices of goods and services are established.
Globalization	Globaliization is the process of integration across world-space arising from the interchange of world views, products, ideas, and other aspects of culture. Advances in transportation and telecommunications infrastructure, including the rise of the telegraph and its posterity the Internet, are major factors in globalization, generating further interdependence of economic and cultural activities. Though scholars place the origins of globalization in modern times, others trace its history long before the European age of discovery and voyages to the New World.
Producer surplus	In mainstream economics, economic surplus (also known as total welfare or Marshallian surplus) refers to two related quantities. Consumer surplus or consumers' surplus is the monetary gain obtained by consumers because they are able to purchase a product for a price that is less than the highest price that they would be willing to pay. Producer surplus or producers' surplus is the amount that producers benefit by selling at a market price that is higher than the least that they would be willing to sell for.
General Agreement on Tariffs and Trade	The General Agreement on Tariffs and Trade was a multilateral agreement regulating international trade. According to its preamble, its purpose was the 'substantial reduction of tariffs and other trade barriers and the elimination of preferences, on a reciprocal and mutually advantageous basis.' It was negotiated during the United Nations Conference on Trade and Employment and was the outcome of the failure of negotiating governments to create the International Trade Organization (ITO).

8. Global Markets in Action,

CHAPTER HIGHLIGHTS & NOTES: KEY TERMS, PEOPLE, PLACES, CONCEPTS

Tariff	A tariff is a tax on imports or exports (an international trade tariff), or a list of prices for such things as rail service, bus routes, and electrical usage (electrical tariff, etc).. The meaning in (1) is now the more common meaning. The meaning in (2) is historically earlier.
World Trade Organization	The World Trade Organization is an organization that intends to supervise and liberalize international trade. The organization officially commenced on 1 January 1995 under the Marrakech Agreement, replacing the General Agreement on Tariffs and Trade (GATT), which commenced in 1948. The organization deals with regulation of trade between participating countries; it provides a framework for negotiating and formalizing trade agreements, and a dispute resolution process aimed at enforcing participant's adherence to World Trade Organization agreements, which are signed by representatives of member governments and ratified by their parliaments. Most of the issues that the World Trade Organization focuses on derive from previous trade negotiations, especially from the Uruguay Round (1986-1994).
Product differentiation	In economics and marketing, product differentiation is the process of distinguishing a product or service from others, to make it more attractive to a particular target market. This involves differentiating it from competitors' products as well as a firm's own products. The concept was proposed by Edward Chamberlin in his 1933 Theory of Monopolistic Competition.
Consumer	A consumer is a person or group of people, such as a household, who are the final users of products or services. The consumer's use is final in the sense that the product is usually not improved by the use.
Deadweight loss	In economics, a deadweight loss is a loss of economic efficiency that can occur when equilibrium for a good or service is not Pareto optimal. Causes of deadweight loss can include monopoly pricing (in the case of artificial scarcity), externalities, taxes or subsidies, and binding price ceilings or floors (including minimum wages). The term deadweight loss may also be referred to as the 'excess burden' of monopoly or taxation.
Import quota	An import quota is a limit on the quantity of a good that can be produced abroad and sold domestically. It is a type of protectionist trade restriction that sets a physical limit on the quantity of a good that can be imported into a country in a given period of time. If a quota is put on a good, less of it is imported.
Subsidies	A subsidy is a form of financial or in kind support extended to an economic sector generally with the aim of promoting economic and social policy. Although commonly extended from Government, the term subsidy can relate to any type of support - for example from NGOs or implicit subsidies. Subsidies come in various forms including: direct (cash grants, interest-free loans) and indirect (tax breaks, insurance, low-interest loans, depreciation write-offs, rent rebates).

8. Global Markets in Action,

CHAPTER HIGHLIGHTS & NOTES: KEY TERMS, PEOPLE, PLACES, CONCEPTS

Voluntary export restraints	A voluntary export restraint or voluntary export restriction is a government imposed limit on the quantity of goods that can be exported out of another country during a specified period of time. Typically Voluntary export restraintss arise when the import-competing industries seek protection from a surge of imports from particular exporting countries. Voluntary export restraintss are then offered by the exporter to appease the importing country and to deter the other party from imposing even more explicit (and less flexible) trade barriers.
Export subsidy	Export subsidy is a government policy to encourage export of goods and discourage sale of goods on the domestic market through direct payments, low-cost loans, tax relief for exporters, or government-financed international advertising. An export subsidy reduces the price paid by foreign importers, which means domestic consumers pay more than foreign consumers. The WTO prohibits most subsidies directly linked to the volume of exports.
Protection	Protection in poker is a bet made with a strong but vulnerable hand, such as top pair when straight or flush draws are possible. The bet forces opponents with draws to either call with insufficient pot odds, or to fold, both of which are profitable for the betting player. By contrast, if he failed to protect his hand, another player could draw out on him at no cost, meaning he gets no value from his made hand.
Dumping	In economics, 'dumping' is a kind of predatory pricing, especially in the context of international trade. It occurs when manufacturers export a product to another country at a price either below the price charged in its home market or below its cost of production.
Diversity	The 'business case for diversity' stem from the progression of the models of diversity within the workplace since the 1960s. The original model for diversity was situated around affirmative action drawing strength from the law and a need to comply with equal opportunity employment objectives. This compliance-based model gave rise to the idea that tokenism was the reason an individual was hired into a company when they differed from the dominant group.
Stability	In probability theory, the stability of a random variable is the property that a linear combination of two independent copies of the variable has the same distribution, up to location and scale parameters. The distributions of random variables having this property are said to be 'stable distributions'. Results available in probability theory show that all possible distributions having this property are members of a four-parameter family of distributions.

8. Global Markets in Action,

CHAPTER QUIZ: KEY TERMS, PEOPLE, PLACES, CONCEPTS

1. In probability theory, the _____ of a random variable is the property that a linear combination of two independent copies of the variable has the same distribution, up to location and scale parameters. The distributions of random variables having this property are said to be 'stable distributions'. Results available in probability theory show that all possible distributions having this property are members of a four-parameter family of distributions.

    a. Cause of death
    b. Ceiling effect
    c. Central limit theorem
    d. Stability

2. An _____ is a limit on the quantity of a good that can be produced abroad and sold domestically. It is a type of protectionist trade restriction that sets a physical limit on the quantity of a good that can be imported into a country in a given period of time. If a quota is put on a good, less of it is imported.

    a. Balanced trade
    b. Balassa index
    c. Import quota
    d. Bilateral trade

3. In economics and marketing, _____ is the process of distinguishing a product or service from others, to make it more attractive to a particular target market. This involves differentiating it from competitors' products as well as a firm's own products. The concept was proposed by Edward Chamberlin in his 1933 Theory of Monopolistic Competition.

    a. Back to school
    b. Product differentiation
    c. Bass diffusion model
    d. Bayesian inference in marketing

4. _____ is an adjective (adverb form: nationally) used to describe a product or publication that is distributed throughout an entire nation, e.g., a _____ magazine. It implies that the item is available for purchase or access anywhere in the country. Comparatively, some products or publications are described as 'local' or 'regional', and are distributed only locally or regionally.

    a. National
    b. Balance of contract
    c. Bridgewater House, Manchester
    d. Bullwhip effect

5. . A _____(s) or voluntary export restriction is a government imposed limit on the quantity of goods that can be exported out of another country during a specified period of time.

    Typically Voluntary export restraintss arise when the import-competing industries seek protection from a surge of imports from particular exporting countries.

8. Global Markets in Action,

CHAPTER QUIZ: KEY TERMS, PEOPLE, PLACES, CONCEPTS

Voluntary export restraintss are then offered by the exporter to appease the importing country and to deter the other party from imposing even more explicit (and less flexible) trade barriers.

a. Balanced trade
b. Voluntary export restraints
c. Banana Framework Agreement
d. Bilateral trade

ANSWER KEY
8. Global Markets in Action,

1. d
2. c
3. b
4. a
5. b

You can take the complete Online Interactive Chapter Practice Test

for 8. Global Markets in Action,
on all key terms, persons, places, and concepts.

No Additional Costs

http://www.Cram101.com

Register, send an email request to Travis.Reese@Cram101.com to get your user Id and password.

Include your customer order number, and ISBN number from your studyguide Retailer.

9. Externalities: Pollution, Education, and Health Care,

CHAPTER OUTLINE: KEY TERMS, PEOPLE, PLACES, CONCEPTS

- Externality
- Income
- Production
- Cost-push inflation
- Marginal cost
- Cost
- Output
- Substitution bias
- Industrial Revolution
- Coase theorem
- Export subsidy
- Property rights
- Market
- Market equilibrium
- Circular flow
- Efficiency
- Pigovian tax
- Air pollution
- Climate change
- Subsidies
- Voucher

9. Externalities: Pollution, Education, and Health Care,
CHAPTER OUTLINE: KEY TERMS, PEOPLE, PLACES, CONCEPTS

- Consumer
- Adverse selection
- Moral hazard
- Economic problem
- Problem
- Public health
- Medicare
- CARE
- Patient Protection and Affordable Care Act
- Plan
- Protection

CHAPTER HIGHLIGHTS & NOTES: KEY TERMS, PEOPLE, PLACES, CONCEPTS

Externality	In economics, an externality is the cost or benefit that affects a party who did not choose to incur that cost or benefit.
	For example, manufacturing activities that cause air pollution impose health and clean-up costs on the whole society, whereas the neighbors of an individual who chooses to fire-proof his home may benefit from a reduced risk of a fire spreading to their own houses. If external costs exist, such as pollution, the producer may choose to produce more of the product than would be produced if the producer were required to pay all associated environmental costs.
Income	Income is the consumption and savings opportunity gained by an entity within a specified timeframe, which is generally expressed in monetary terms. However, for households and individuals, 'income is the sum of all the wages, salaries, profits, interests payments, rents and other forms of earnings received... in a given period of time.'

9. Externalities: Pollution, Education, and Health Care,

CHAPTER HIGHLIGHTS & NOTES: KEY TERMS, PEOPLE, PLACES, CONCEPTS

	In the field of public economics, the term may refer to the accumulation of both monetary and non-monetary consumption ability, with the former (monetary) being used as a proxy for total income.
Production	Production is a process of combining various material inputs and immaterial inputs in order to make something for consumption (the output). It is the act of creating output, a good or service which has value and contributes to the utility of individuals. Economic well-being is created in a production process, meaning all economic activities that aim directly or indirectly to satisfy human needs.
Cost-push inflation	Cost-push inflation is an alleged type of inflation caused by substantial increases in the cost of important goods or services where no suitable alternative is available. A situation that has been often cited of this was the oil crisis of the 1970s, which some economists see as a major cause of the inflation experienced in the Western world in that decade. It is argued that this inflation resulted from increases in the cost of petroleum imposed by the member states of OPEC. Since petroleum is so important to industrialised economies, a large increase in its price can lead to the increase in the price of most products, raising the inflation rate.
Marginal cost	In economics and finance, marginal cost is the change in the total cost that arises when the quantity produced has an increment by unit. That is, it is the cost of producing one more unit of a good. In general terms, marginal cost at each level of production includes any additional costs required to produce the next unit.
Cost	In production, research, retail, and accounting, a cost is the value of money that has been used up to produce something, and hence is not available for use anymore. In business, the cost may be one of acquisition, in which case the amount of money expended to acquire it is counted as cost. In this case, money is the input that is gone in order to acquire the thing.
Output	Output in economics is the 'quantity of goods or services produced in a given time period, by a firm, industry, or country,' whether consumed or used for further production. The concept of national output is absolutely essential in the field of macroeconomics. It is national output that makes a country rich, not large amounts of money.
Substitution bias	Substitution bias describes a bias in economics index numbers arising from tendency to purchase inexpensive substitutes for expensive items when prices change.
	Substitution bias occurs when two or more items experience a change of price relative to each other. Consumers will consume more of the now comparatively inexpensive good and less of the now relatively more expensive good.
Industrial Revolution	The Industrial Revolution was the transition to new manufacturing processes in the period from about 1760 to sometime between 1820 and 1840.

9. Externalities: Pollution, Education, and Health Care,

CHAPTER HIGHLIGHTS & NOTES: KEY TERMS, PEOPLE, PLACES, CONCEPTS

	This transition included going from hand production methods to machines, new chemical manufacturing and iron production processes, improved efficiency of water power, the increasing use of steam power and the development of machine tools. It also included the change from wood and other bio-fuels to coal.
	Textiles were the dominant industry of the Industrial Revolution in terms of employment, value of output and capital invested.
Coase theorem	In law and economics, the Coase theorem describes the economic efficiency of an economic allocation or outcome in the presence of externalities. The theorem states that if trade in an externality is possible and there are sufficiently low transaction costs, bargaining will lead to an efficient outcome regardless of the initial allocation of property. In practice, obstacles to bargaining or poorly defined property rights can prevent Coasian bargaining.
Export subsidy	Export subsidy is a government policy to encourage export of goods and discourage sale of goods on the domestic market through direct payments, low-cost loans, tax relief for exporters, or government-financed international advertising. An export subsidy reduces the price paid by foreign importers, which means domestic consumers pay more than foreign consumers. The WTO prohibits most subsidies directly linked to the volume of exports.
Property rights	Property rights are theoretical constructs in economics for determining how a resource is used and owned. Resources can be owned (the subject of property) by individuals, associations or governments. Property rights can be viewed as an attribute of an economic good.
Market	A market is one of the many varieties of systems, institutions, procedures, social relations and infrastructures whereby parties engage in exchange. While parties may exchange goods and services by barter, most markets rely on sellers offering their goods or services (including labor) in exchange for money from buyers. It can be said that a market is the process by which the prices of goods and services are established.
Market equilibrium	In economics, economic equilibrium is a state where economic forces such as supply and demand are balanced and in the absence of external influences the values of economic variables will not change. For example, in the standard text-book model of perfect competition, equilibrium occurs at the point at which quantity demanded and quantity supplied are equal. Market equilibrium in this case refers to a condition where a market price is established through competition such that the amount of goods or services sought by buyers is equal to the amount of goods or services produced by sellers.
Circular flow	In economics, the terms circular flow of income or circular flow refer to a simple economic model which describes the reciprocal circulation of income between producers and consumers.

9. Externalities: Pollution, Education, and Health Care,

CHAPTER HIGHLIGHTS & NOTES: KEY TERMS, PEOPLE, PLACES, CONCEPTS

	In the circular flow model, the inter-dependent entities of producer and consumer are referred to as 'firms' and 'households' respectively and provide each other with factors in order to facilitate the flow of income. Firms provide consumers with goods and services in exchange for consumer expenditure and 'factors of production' from households.
Efficiency	The relative efficiency of two procedures is the ratio of their efficiencies, although often this term is used where the comparison is made between a given procedure and a notional 'best possible' procedure. The efficiencies and the relative efficiency of two procedures theoretically depend on the sample size available for the given procedure, but it is often possible to use the asymptotic relative efficiency as the principal comparison measure. Efficiencies are often defined using the variance or mean square error as the measure of desirability.
Pigovian tax	A Pigovian tax is a tax applied to a market activity that is generating negative externalities (costs for somebody else). The tax is intended to correct an inefficient market outcome, and does so by being set equal to the negative externalities. In the presence of negative externalities, the social cost of a market activity is not covered by the private cost of the activity.
Air pollution	Air pollution is the introduction of chemicals, particulates, biological materials, or other harmful materials into the Earth's atmosphere, possibly causing disease, death to humans, damage to other living organisms such as food crops, or the natural or built environment. The atmosphere is a complex natural gaseous system that is essential to support life on planet Earth. Stratospheric ozone depletion due to air pollution has long been recognized as a threat to human health as well as to the Earth's ecosystems.
Climate change	Climate change is a significant and lasting change in the statistical distribution of weather patterns over periods ranging from decades to millions of years. It may be a change in average weather conditions, or in the distribution of weather around the average conditions (i.e., more or fewer extreme weather events). Climate change is caused by factors such as biotic processes, variations in solar radiation received by Earth, plate tectonics, and volcanic eruptions.
Subsidies	A subsidy is a form of financial or in kind support extended to an economic sector generally with the aim of promoting economic and social policy. Although commonly extended from Government, the term subsidy can relate to any type of support - for example from NGOs or implicit subsidies. Subsidies come in various forms including: direct (cash grants, interest-free loans) and indirect (tax breaks, insurance, low-interest loans, depreciation write-offs, rent rebates).
Voucher	A voucher is a bond of the redeemable transaction type which is worth a certain monetary value and which may be spent only for specific reasons or on specific goods. Examples include (but are not limited to) housing, travel, and food vouchers.

9. Externalities: Pollution, Education, and Health Care,

CHAPTER HIGHLIGHTS & NOTES: KEY TERMS, PEOPLE, PLACES, CONCEPTS

Consumer	A consumer is a person or group of people, such as a household, who are the final users of products or services. The consumer's use is final in the sense that the product is usually not improved by the use.
Adverse selection	Adverse selection, anti-selection, or negative selection is a term used in economics, insurance, risk management, and statistics. It refers to a market process in which undesired results occur when buyers and sellers have asymmetric information (access to different information); the 'bad' products or services are more likely to be selected. For example, a bank that sets one price for all of its checking account customers runs the risk of being adversely selected against by its low-balance, high-activity (and hence least profitable) customers.
Moral hazard	In economic theory, a moral hazard is a situation where a party will have a tendency to take risks because the costs that could result will not be felt by the party taking the risk. In other words, it is a tendency to be more willing to take a risk, knowing that the potential costs or burdens of taking such risk will be borne, in whole or in part, by others. A moral hazard may occur where the actions of one party may change to the detriment of another after a financial transaction has taken place.
Economic problem	The economic problem, sometimes called the basic, central or fundamental economic problem, is one of the fundamental economic theories in the operation of any economy. It asserts that there is scarcity, or that the finite resources available are insufficient to satisfy all human wants and needs. The problem then becomes how to determine what is to be produced and how the factors of production (such as capital and labor) are to be allocated.
Problem	A problem, which can be caused for different reasons, and, if solvable, can usually be solved in a number of different ways, is defined in a number of different ways. This is determined by the context in which a said problems is defined. When discussed, a problem can be argued in multiple ways.
Public health	Public health is 'the science and art of preventing disease, prolonging life and promoting health through the organized efforts and informed choices of society, organizations, public and private, communities and individuals.' It is concerned with threats to health based on population health analysis. The population in question can be as small as a handful of people, or as large as all the inhabitants of several continents (for instance, in the case of a pandemic). The dimensions of health can encompass 'a state of complete physical, mental and social well-being and not merely the absence of disease or infirmity', as defined by the United Nations' World Health Organization.
Medicare	Medicare is a publicly funded universal health care scheme in Australia. Operated by the government authority Medicare Australia, Medicare is the primary funder of health care in Australia, funding primary health care for Australian citizens and permanent residents (except for those on Norfolk Island).

9. Externalities: Pollution, Education, and Health Care,

CHAPTER HIGHLIGHTS & NOTES: KEY TERMS, PEOPLE, PLACES, CONCEPTS

CARE	CARE is a major international humanitarian agency delivering broad-spectrum emergency relief and long-term international development projects. Founded in 1945, CARE is nonsectarian, non-partisan, and non-governmental. It is one of the largest and oldest humanitarian aid organizations focused on fighting global poverty.
Patient Protection and Affordable Care Act	The Patient Protection and Affordable Care Act, commonly called the Affordable Care Act (ACA) or Obamacare, is a United States federal statute enacted by President Barack Obama on March 23, 2010. Together with the Health Care and Education Reconciliation Act amendment, it represents the most significant regulatory overhaul of the U.S. healthcare system since the passage of Medicare and Medicaid in 1965. Under the act, hospitals and primary physicians would transform their practices financially, technologically, and clinically to drive better health outcomes, lower costs, and improve their methods of distribution and accessibility. The Affordable Care Act was intended to increase health insurance quality and affordability, lower the uninsured rate by expanding insurance coverage and reduce the costs of healthcare. It introduced mechanisms including mandates, subsidies and insurance exchanges.
Plan	A plan is typically any diagram or list of steps with timing and resources, used to achieve an objective. See also strategy. It is commonly understood as a temporal set of intended actions through which one expects to achieve a goal.
Protection	Protection in poker is a bet made with a strong but vulnerable hand, such as top pair when straight or flush draws are possible. The bet forces opponents with draws to either call with insufficient pot odds, or to fold, both of which are profitable for the betting player. By contrast, if he failed to protect his hand, another player could draw out on him at no cost, meaning he gets no value from his made hand.

9. Externalities: Pollution, Education, and Health Care,

CHAPTER QUIZ: KEY TERMS, PEOPLE, PLACES, CONCEPTS

1. The _____, commonly called the Affordable Care Act (ACA) or Obamacare, is a United States federal statute enacted by President Barack Obama on March 23, 2010. Together with the Health Care and Education Reconciliation Act amendment, it represents the most significant regulatory overhaul of the U.S. healthcare system since the passage of Medicare and Medicaid in 1965. Under the act, hospitals and primary physicians would transform their practices financially, technologically, and clinically to drive better health outcomes, lower costs, and improve their methods of distribution and accessibility.

    The Affordable Care Act was intended to increase health insurance quality and affordability, lower the uninsured rate by expanding insurance coverage and reduce the costs of healthcare. It introduced mechanisms including mandates, subsidies and insurance exchanges.

    a. Patient Protection and Affordable Care Act
    b. Benevolent Organisation for Development, Health and Insight
    c. Bethlehem Association
    d. Beyond Sport

2. _____ is a significant and lasting change in the statistical distribution of weather patterns over periods ranging from decades to millions of years. It may be a change in average weather conditions, or in the distribution of weather around the average conditions (i.e., more or fewer extreme weather events). _____ is caused by factors such as biotic processes, variations in solar radiation received by Earth, plate tectonics, and volcanic eruptions.

    a. Climate change
    b. Carbon Clear
    c. Carbon credit
    d. Carbon finance

3. A _____, which can be caused for different reasons, and, if solvable, can usually be solved in a number of different ways, is defined in a number of different ways. This is determined by the context in which a said _____s is defined. When discussed, a _____ can be argued in multiple ways.

    a. 100 Best Workplaces in Europe
    b. Career portfolio
    c. Problem
    d. Commercial Product Assurance

4. . _____ is a process of combining various material inputs and immaterial inputs in order to make something for consumption (the output). It is the act of creating output, a good or service which has value and contributes to the utility of individuals. Economic well-being is created in a _____ process, meaning all economic activities that aim directly or indirectly to satisfy human needs.

    a. Capacity utilization
    b. Constant elasticity of substitution
    c. Constant elasticity of transformation

9. Externalities: Pollution, Education, and Health Care,

CHAPTER QUIZ: KEY TERMS, PEOPLE, PLACES, CONCEPTS

5. In economics, an _____ is the cost or benefit that affects a party who did not choose to incur that cost or benefit.

For example, manufacturing activities that cause air pollution impose health and clean-up costs on the whole society, whereas the neighbors of an individual who chooses to fire-proof his home may benefit from a reduced risk of a fire spreading to their own houses. If external costs exist, such as pollution, the producer may choose to produce more of the product than would be produced if the producer were required to pay all associated environmental costs.

a. Bank of Natural Capital
b. Externality
c. Boat sharing
d. Buy Quiet

ANSWER KEY
9. Externalities: Pollution, Education, and Health Care,

1. a
2. a
3. c
4. d
5. b

You can take the complete Online Interactive Chapter Practice Test

for 9. Externalities: Pollution, Education, and Health Care,
on all key terms, persons, places, and concepts.

No Additional Costs

http://www.Cram101.com

Register, send an email request to Travis.Reese@Cram101.com to get your user Id and password.

Include your customer order number, and ISBN number from your studyguide Retailer.

10. Production and Cost,

CHAPTER OUTLINE: KEY TERMS, PEOPLE, PLACES, CONCEPTS

	Business cycle
	Cost-push inflation
	Cost
	Profit
	Executive officer
	Explicit cost
	Implicit cost
	Interest
	Long
	Long run
	Income
	Marginal product
	Marginal return
	Product
	Average
	Total cost
	Marginal cost
	Average cost
	Average variable cost
	Cost curve
	Factor

10. Production and Cost,
CHAPTER OUTLINE: KEY TERMS, PEOPLE, PLACES, CONCEPTS

_____ | Factor price
_____ | Perfect competition
_____ | Price
_____ | Price level
_____ | Product differentiation
_____ | Competition
_____ | Factors of production
_____ | Production
_____ | Technological change
_____ | Economies of scale
_____ | Capital
_____ | Size
_____ | Specialization
_____ | Diseconomies of scale
_____ | Returns

10. Production and Cost,

CHAPTER HIGHLIGHTS & NOTES: KEY TERMS, PEOPLE, PLACES, CONCEPTS

Business cycle	The term business cycle refers to economy-wide fluctuations in production, trade and economic activity in general over several months or years in an economy organized on free-enterprise principles.
	The business cycle is the upward and downward movements of levels of GDP (gross domestic product) and refers to the period of expansions and contractions in the level of economic activities (business fluctuations) around its long-term growth trend.
	These fluctuations occur around a long-term growth trend, and typically involve shifts over time between periods of relatively rapid economic growth (an expansion or boom), and periods of relative stagnation or decline (a contraction or recession).
Cost-push inflation	Cost-push inflation is an alleged type of inflation caused by substantial increases in the cost of important goods or services where no suitable alternative is available. A situation that has been often cited of this was the oil crisis of the 1970s, which some economists see as a major cause of the inflation experienced in the Western world in that decade. It is argued that this inflation resulted from increases in the cost of petroleum imposed by the member states of OPEC. Since petroleum is so important to industrialised economies, a large increase in its price can lead to the increase in the price of most products, raising the inflation rate.
Cost	In production, research, retail, and accounting, a cost is the value of money that has been used up to produce something, and hence is not available for use anymore. In business, the cost may be one of acquisition, in which case the amount of money expended to acquire it is counted as cost. In this case, money is the input that is gone in order to acquire the thing.
Profit	In neoclassical microeconomic theory, the term profit has two related but distinct meanings. Economic profit is similar to accounting profit but smaller because it reflects the total opportunity costs (both explicit and implicit) of a venture to an investor. Normal profit refers to a situation in which the economic profit is zero.
Executive officer	An executive officer is generally a person responsible for running an organization, although the exact nature of the role varies depending on the organization.
Explicit cost	An explicit cost is a direct payment made to others in the course of running a business, such as wage, rent and materials, as opposed to implicit costs, which are those where no actual payment is made. It is possible still to underestimate these costs, however: for example, pension contributions and other 'perks' must be taken into account when considering the cost of labour.
	Explicit costs are taken into account along with implicit ones when considering economic profit.

10. Production and Cost,

CHAPTER HIGHLIGHTS & NOTES: KEY TERMS, PEOPLE, PLACES, CONCEPTS

Implicit cost	In economics, an implicit cost, also called an imputed cost, implied cost, or notional cost, is the opportunity cost equal to what a firm must give up in order to use factors which it neither purchases nor hires. It is the opposite of an explicit cost, which is borne directly. In other words, an implicit cost is any cost that results from using an asset instead of renting, selling, or lending it.
Interest	Interest is a fee paid by a borrower of assets to the owner as a form of compensation for the use of the assets. It is most commonly the price paid for the use of borrowed money, or money earned by deposited funds. When money is borrowed, interest is typically paid to the lender as a percentage of the principal, the amount owed to the lender.
Long	Long/short equity is an investment strategy generally associated with hedge funds, and more recently certain progressive traditional asset managers. It involves buying long equities that are expected to increase in value and selling short equities that are expected to decrease in value. This is different from the risk reversal strategies where investors will simultaneously buy a call option and sell a put option to simulate being long in a stock.
Long run	In microeconomics, the long run is the conceptual time period in which there are no fixed factors of production as to changing the output level by changing the capital stock or by entering or leaving an industry. The long run contrasts with the short run, in which some factors are variable and others are fixed, constraining entry or exit from an industry. In macroeconomics, the long run is the period when the general price level, contractual wage rates, and expectations adjust fully to the state of the economy, in contrast to the short run when these variables may not fully adjust.
Income	Income is the consumption and savings opportunity gained by an entity within a specified timeframe, which is generally expressed in monetary terms. However, for households and individuals, 'income is the sum of all the wages, salaries, profits, interests payments, rents and other forms of earnings received... in a given period of time.' In the field of public economics, the term may refer to the accumulation of both monetary and non-monetary consumption ability, with the former (monetary) being used as a proxy for total income.
Marginal product	In economics and in particular neoclassical economics, the marginal product or marginal physical product of an input is the extra output that can be produced by using one more unit of the input (for instance, the difference in output when a firm's labor usage is increased from five to six units), assuming that the quantities of no other inputs to production change. The marginal product of a given input can be expressed as $MP = \dfrac{\Delta Y}{\Delta X}$ where ΔX is the change in the firm's use of the input (conventionally a one-unit change) and

10. Production and Cost,

CHAPTER HIGHLIGHTS & NOTES: KEY TERMS, PEOPLE, PLACES, CONCEPTS

	ΔY is the change in quantity of output produced. Note that the quantity Y of the 'product' is typically defined ignoring external costs and benefits.
Marginal return	Marginal return refers to the additional output resulting from a one unit increase in the use of variable inputs, while other inputs are held constant.
Product	In marketing, a product is anything that can be offered to a market that might satisfy a want or need. In retailing, products are called merchandise. In manufacturing, products are bought as raw materials and sold as finished goods.
Average	In colloquial language average usually refers to the sum of a list of numbers divided by the size of the list, in other words the arithmetic mean. However, the word 'average' can be used to refer to the median, the mode, or some other central or typical value. In statistics, these are all known as measures of central tendency.
Total cost	In economics, and cost accounting, total cost describes the total economic cost of production and is made up of variable costs, which vary according to the quantity of a good produced and include inputs such as labor and raw materials, plus fixed costs, which are independent of the quantity of a good produced and include inputs (capital) that cannot be varied in the short term, such as buildings and machinery. Total cost in economics includes the total opportunity cost of each factor of production as part of its fixed or variable costs. The rate at which total cost changes as the amount produced changes is called marginal cost.
Marginal cost	In economics and finance, marginal cost is the change in the total cost that arises when the quantity produced has an increment by unit. That is, it is the cost of producing one more unit of a good. In general terms, marginal cost at each level of production includes any additional costs required to produce the next unit.
Average cost	In economics, average cost or unit cost is equal to total cost divided by the number of goods produced. It is also equal to the sum of average variable costs (total variable costs divided by Q) plus average fixed costs (total fixed costs divided by Q). Average costs may be dependent on the time period considered (increasing production may be expensive or impossible in the short term, for example).
Average variable cost	In economics, average variable cost is a firm's variable costs (labor, electricity, etc). divided by the quantity (Q) of output produced. Variable costs are those costs which vary with output.
Cost curve	In economics, a cost curve is a graph of the costs of production as a function of total quantity produced. In a free market economy, productively efficient firms use these curves to find the optimal point of production (minimizing cost), and profit maximizing firms can use them to decide output quantities to achieve those aims.

10. Production and Cost,

CHAPTER HIGHLIGHTS & NOTES: KEY TERMS, PEOPLE, PLACES, CONCEPTS

Factor	A factor, Latin for 'doer, maker', is a mercantile fiduciary who receives and sells goods on commission (called factorage), transacting business in his own name and not disclosing his principal, and historically with his seat at a factory (trading post). A factor differs from a commission merchant in that a factor takes possession of goods (or documents of title representing goods) on consignment, whereas a commission merchant sells goods not in his possession on the basis of samples. Most modern factor business is in the textile field, but factors are also used to a great extent in the shoe, furniture, hardware, and other industries, and the trade areas in which factors operate have increased.
Factor price	In economic theory, the price of a finished item affects the factors of production, the various costs and incentives of producing it, so as to 'attract' it toward a theoretical Factor price. Simply put, factor price is why the price of an item tends to approach the cost of producing it. There has been much debate as to what determines factor prices.
Perfect competition	In economic theory, perfect competition describes markets such that no participants are large enough to have the market power to set the price of a homogeneous product. Because the conditions for perfect competition are strict, there are few if any perfectly competitive markets. Still, buyers and sellers in some auction-type markets, say for commodities or some financial assets, may approximate the concept.
Price	In ordinary usage, price is the quantity of payment or compensation given by one party to another in return for goods or services. In modern economies, prices are generally expressed in units of some form of currency. (For commodities, they are expressed as currency per unit weight of the commodity, e.g. euros per kilogram).
Price level	The general price level is a hypothetical measure of overall prices for some set of goods and services, in a given region during a given interval, normalized relative to some base set. Typically, a price level is approximated with a price index.
Product differentiation	In economics and marketing, product differentiation is the process of distinguishing a product or service from others, to make it more attractive to a particular target market. This involves differentiating it from competitors' products as well as a firm's own products. The concept was proposed by Edward Chamberlin in his 1933 Theory of Monopolistic Competition.
Competition	In economics, competition is the rivalry among sellers trying to achieve such goals as increasing profits, market share, and sales volume by varying the elements of the marketing mix: price, product, distribution, and promotion.

10. Production and Cost,

CHAPTER HIGHLIGHTS & NOTES: KEY TERMS, PEOPLE, PLACES, CONCEPTS

	Merriam-Webster defines competition in business as 'the effort of two or more parties acting independently to secure the business of a third party by offering the most favorable terms.' It was described by Adam Smith in The Wealth of Nations (1776) and later economists as allocating productive resources to their most highly-valued uses and encouraging efficiency. Smith and other classical economists before Cournot were referring to price and non-price rivalry among producers to sell their goods on best terms by bidding of buyers, not necessarily to a large number of sellers nor to a market in final equilibrium.
Factors of production	In economics, factors of production are the inputs to the production process. Finished goods are the output. Input determines the quantity of output i.e. output depends upon input.
Production	Production is a process of combining various material inputs and immaterial inputs in order to make something for consumption (the output). It is the act of creating output, a good or service which has value and contributes to the utility of individuals. Economic well-being is created in a production process, meaning all economic activities that aim directly or indirectly to satisfy human needs.
Technological change	Technological change is a term that is used to describe the overall process of invention, innovation and diffusion of technology or processes. The term is synonymous with technological development, technological achievement, and technological progress. In essence TC is the invention of a technology (or a process), the continuous process of improving a technology (in which it often becomes cheaper) and its diffusion throughout industry or society.
Economies of scale	In microeconomics, economies of scale are the cost advantages that enterprises obtain due to size, output, or scale of operation, with cost per unit of output generally decreasing with increasing scale as fixed costs are spread out over more units of output. Often operational efficiency is also greater with increasing scale, leading to lower variable cost as well. Economies of scale apply to a variety of organizational and business situations and at various levels, such as a business or manufacturing unit, plant or an entire enterprise.
Capital	In economics, capital goods, real capital, or capital assets are already-produced durable goods or any non-financial asset that is used in production of goods or services. Capital goods are not significantly consumed in the production process though they may depreciate. How a capital good or is maintained or returned to its pre-production state varies with the type of capital involved.
Size	In statistics, the size of a test is the probability of falsely rejecting the null hypothesis. It is denoted by the Greek letter a (alpha). For a simple hypothesis, $\alpha = P(\text{test rejects } H_0 \mid H_0)$.

10. Production and Cost,

CHAPTER HIGHLIGHTS & NOTES: KEY TERMS, PEOPLE, PLACES, CONCEPTS

Specialization	Specialization is the separation of tasks within a system. In a multicellular creature, cells are specialized for functions such as bone construction or oxygen transport. In capitalist societies, individual workers specialize for functions such as building construction or gasoline transport.
Diseconomies of scale	Diseconomies of scale are the forces that cause larger firms and governments to produce goods and services at increased per-unit costs. The concept is the opposite of economies of scale.
Returns	Returns, in economics and political economy, are the distributions or payments awarded to the various suppliers of the factors of production.

CHAPTER QUIZ: KEY TERMS, PEOPLE, PLACES, CONCEPTS

1. In ordinary usage, _____ is the quantity of payment or compensation given by one party to another in return for goods or services.

   In modern economies, _____s are generally expressed in units of some form of currency. (For commodities, they are expressed as currency per unit weight of the commodity, e.g. euros per kilogram).

   a. Back to school
   b. Backward invention
   c. Bass diffusion model
   d. Price

2. In economics and marketing, _____ is the process of distinguishing a product or service from others, to make it more attractive to a particular target market. This involves differentiating it from competitors' products as well as a firm's own products. The concept was proposed by Edward Chamberlin in his 1933 Theory of Monopolistic Competition.

   a. Product differentiation
   b. Backward invention
   c. Bass diffusion model
   d. Bayesian inference in marketing

3. . An _____ is a direct payment made to others in the course of running a business, such as wage, rent and materials, as opposed to implicit costs, which are those where no actual payment is made. It is possible still to underestimate these costs, however: for example, pension contributions and other 'perks' must be taken into account when considering the cost of labour.

   _____s are taken into account along with implicit ones when considering economic profit.

10. Production and Cost,

CHAPTER QUIZ: KEY TERMS, PEOPLE, PLACES, CONCEPTS

   a. Business mileage reimbursement rate
   b. Cost
   c. Explicit cost
   d. Cost curve

4. The term _____ refers to economy-wide fluctuations in production, trade and economic activity in general over several months or years in an economy organized on free-enterprise principles.

   The _____ is the upward and downward movements of levels of GDP (gross domestic product) and refers to the period of expansions and contractions in the level of economic activities (business fluctuations) around its long-term growth trend.

   These fluctuations occur around a long-term growth trend, and typically involve shifts over time between periods of relatively rapid economic growth (an expansion or boom), and periods of relative stagnation or decline (a contraction or recession).

   a. Bad bank
   b. Bank failure
   c. Jewish Social Democratic Party
   d. Business cycle

5. _____ is an alleged type of inflation caused by substantial increases in the cost of important goods or services where no suitable alternative is available. A situation that has been often cited of this was the oil crisis of the 1970s, which some economists see as a major cause of the inflation experienced in the Western world in that decade. It is argued that this inflation resulted from increases in the cost of petroleum imposed by the member states of OPEC. Since petroleum is so important to industrialised economies, a large increase in its price can lead to the increase in the price of most products, raising the inflation rate.

   a. Base effect
   b. Built-in inflation
   c. Chronic inflation
   d. Cost-push inflation

ANSWER KEY
10. Production and Cost,

1. d
2. a
3. c
4. d
5. d

You can take the complete Online Interactive Chapter Practice Test

for 10. Production and Cost,
on all key terms, persons, places, and concepts.

No Additional Costs

http://www.Cram101.com

Register, send an email request to Travis.Reese@Cram101.com to get your user Id and password.

Include your customer order number, and ISBN number from your studyguide Retailer.

11. Perfect Competition,

CHAPTER OUTLINE: KEY TERMS, PEOPLE, PLACES, CONCEPTS

- Monopolistic competition
- Monopoly
- Oligopoly
- Perfect competition
- Market
- Outcome
- Business cycle
- Economic profit
- Marginal revenue
- Demand
- Total cost
- Total revenue
- Break-even
- Cost
- Law of supply
- Shutdown
- Supply curve
- Short
- Short run
- Supply
- Cost-push inflation

11. Perfect Competition,

CHAPTER OUTLINE: KEY TERMS, PEOPLE, PLACES, CONCEPTS

	Long
	Good
	Hong
	Index
	Exit
	Incentive
	Income
	Technological change
	Competitive Market
	Circular flow
	Efficiency
	Factor
	Competition
	Consumer
	Production

11. Perfect Competition,

CHAPTER HIGHLIGHTS & NOTES: KEY TERMS, PEOPLE, PLACES, CONCEPTS

Monopolistic competition	Monopolistic competition is a type of imperfect competition such that many producers sell products that are differentiated from one another and hence are not perfect substitutes. In monopolistic competition, a firm takes the prices charged by its rivals as given and ignores the impact of its own prices on the prices of other firms. In the presence of coercive government, monopolistic competition will fall into government-granted monopoly.
Monopoly	A monopoly (from Greek monos μ???? + polein p??e?? (to sell)) exists when a specific person or enterprise is the only supplier of a particular commodity (this contrasts with a monopsony which relates to a single entity's control of a market to purchase a good or service, and with oligopoly which consists of a few entities dominating an industry). Monopolies are thus characterized by a lack of economic competition to produce the good or service and a lack of viable substitute goods. The verb 'monopolize' refers to the process by which a company gains the ability to raise prices or exclude competitors.
Oligopoly	An oligopoly is a market form in which a market or industry is dominated by a small number of sellers . Oligopolies can result from various forms of collusion which reduce competition and lead to higher prices for consumers. With few sellers, each oligopolist is likely to be aware of the actions of the others.
Perfect competition	In economic theory, perfect competition describes markets such that no participants are large enough to have the market power to set the price of a homogeneous product. Because the conditions for perfect competition are strict, there are few if any perfectly competitive markets. Still, buyers and sellers in some auction-type markets, say for commodities or some financial assets, may approximate the concept.
Market	A market is one of the many varieties of systems, institutions, procedures, social relations and infrastructures whereby parties engage in exchange. While parties may exchange goods and services by barter, most markets rely on sellers offering their goods or services (including labor) in exchange for money from buyers. It can be said that a market is the process by which the prices of goods and services are established.
Outcome	In game theory, an outcome is a set of moves or strategies taken by the players, or it is their payoffs resulting from the actions or strategies taken by all players. The two are complementary in that, given knowledge of the set of strategies of all players, the final state of the game is known, as are any relevant payoffs. In a game where chance or a random event is involved, the outcome is not known from only the set of strategies, but is only realized when the random event(s) are realized.
Business cycle	The term business cycle refers to economy-wide fluctuations in production, trade and economic activity in general over several months or years in an economy organized on free-enterprise principles.

11. Perfect Competition,

CHAPTER HIGHLIGHTS & NOTES: KEY TERMS, PEOPLE, PLACES, CONCEPTS

	The business cycle is the upward and downward movements of levels of GDP (gross domestic product) and refers to the period of expansions and contractions in the level of economic activities (business fluctuations) around its long-term growth trend. These fluctuations occur around a long-term growth trend, and typically involve shifts over time between periods of relatively rapid economic growth (an expansion or boom), and periods of relative stagnation or decline (a contraction or recession).
Economic profit	In neoclassical microeconomic theory, the term profit has two related but distinct meanings. Economic profit is similar to accounting profit but smaller because it reflects the total opportunity costs (both explicit and implicit) of a venture to an investor. Normal profit refers to a situation in which the economic profit is zero.
Marginal revenue	In microeconomics, marginal revenue is the additional revenue that will be generated by increasing product sales by 1 unit. It can also be described as the unit revenue the last item sold has generated for the firm. In a perfectly competitive market, the additional revenue generated by selling an additional unit of a good is equal to the price the firm is able to charge the buyer of the good.
Demand	In economics, demand for a good or service is an entire listing of the quantity of the good or service that a market would choose to buy, for every possible market price of the good or service. (Note: This distinguishes 'demand' from 'quantity demanded', where demand is a listing or graphing of quantity demanded at each possible price. In contrast to demand, quantity demanded is the exact quantity demanded at a certain price.
Total cost	In economics, and cost accounting, total cost describes the total economic cost of production and is made up of variable costs, which vary according to the quantity of a good produced and include inputs such as labor and raw materials, plus fixed costs, which are independent of the quantity of a good produced and include inputs (capital) that cannot be varied in the short term, such as buildings and machinery. Total cost in economics includes the total opportunity cost of each factor of production as part of its fixed or variable costs. The rate at which total cost changes as the amount produced changes is called marginal cost.
Total revenue	Total revenue is the total receipts of a firm from the sale of any given quantity of a product. It can be calculated as the selling price of the firm's product times the quantity sold, i.e. total revenue = price × quantity, or letting TR be the total revenue function: $$TR(Q) = P(Q) \times Q$$

11. Perfect Competition,

CHAPTER HIGHLIGHTS & NOTES: KEY TERMS, PEOPLE, PLACES, CONCEPTS

Break-even	Break-even is the point of balance between making either a profit or a loss. The term originates in finance, but the concept has been applied widely since.
Cost	In production, research, retail, and accounting, a cost is the value of money that has been used up to produce something, and hence is not available for use anymore. In business, the cost may be one of acquisition, in which case the amount of money expended to acquire it is counted as cost. In this case, money is the input that is gone in order to acquire the thing.
Law of supply	The law of supply is a fundamental principle of economic theory which states that, all else equal, an increase in price results in an increase in quantity supplied. In other words, there is a direct relationship between price and quantity: quantities respond in the same direction as price changes. This means that producers are willing to offer more products for sale on the market at higher prices by increasing production as a way of increasing profits.
Shutdown	In economics, a firm will choose to implement a shutdown of production when the revenue received from the sale of the goods or services produced cannot even cover the variable costs of production. In that situation, the firm will experience a higher loss when it produces, compared to not producing at all. Technically, shutdown occurs if marginal revenue is below average variable cost at the profit-maximizing output.
Supply curve	In microeconomics, supply and demand is an economic model of price determination in a market. It concludes that in a competitive market, the unit price for a particular good will vary until it settles at a point where the quantity demanded by consumers (at current price) will equal the quantity supplied by producers (at current price), resulting in an economic equilibrium for price and quantity. The four basic laws of supply and demand are:•If demand increases (demand curve shifts to the right) and supply remains unchanged, a shortage occurs, leading to a higher equilibrium price.•If demand decreases (demand curve shifts to the left) supply remains unchanged, a surplus occurs, leading to a lower equilibrium price.•If demand remains unchanged and supply increases (supply curve shifts to the right), a surplus occurs, leading to a lower equilibrium price.•If demand remains unchanged and supply decreases (supply curve shifts to the left), a shortage occurs, leading to a higher equilibrium price.
Short	In finance, short selling (also known as shorting or going short) is the practice of selling securities or other financial instruments that are not currently owned, and subsequently repurchasing them . In the event of an interim price decline, the short seller will profit, since the cost of (re)purchase will be less than the proceeds which were received upon the initial (short) sale. Conversely, the short position will be closed out at a loss in the event that the price of a shorted instrument should rise prior to repurchase.

11. Perfect Competition,

CHAPTER HIGHLIGHTS & NOTES: KEY TERMS, PEOPLE, PLACES, CONCEPTS

Short run	In microeconomics, the long run is the conceptual time period in which there are no fixed factors of production as to changing the output level by changing the capital stock or by entering or leaving an industry. The long run contrasts with the short run, in which some factors are variable and others are fixed, constraining entry or exit from an industry. In macroeconomics, the long run is the period when the general price level, contractual wage rates, and expectations adjust fully to the state of the economy, in contrast to the short run when these variables may not fully adjust.
Supply	In economics, supply refers to the amount of a product that producers and firms are willing to sell at a given price all other factors being held constant. Usually, supply is plotted as a supply curve showing the relationship of price to the amount of product businesses are willing to sell.
Cost-push inflation	Cost-push inflation is an alleged type of inflation caused by substantial increases in the cost of important goods or services where no suitable alternative is available. A situation that has been often cited of this was the oil crisis of the 1970s, which some economists see as a major cause of the inflation experienced in the Western world in that decade. It is argued that this inflation resulted from increases in the cost of petroleum imposed by the member states of OPEC. Since petroleum is so important to industrialised economies, a large increase in its price can lead to the increase in the price of most products, raising the inflation rate.
Long	Long/short equity is an investment strategy generally associated with hedge funds, and more recently certain progressive traditional asset managers. It involves buying long equities that are expected to increase in value and selling short equities that are expected to decrease in value. This is different from the risk reversal strategies where investors will simultaneously buy a call option and sell a put option to simulate being long in a stock.
Good	In economics, a good is a material that satisfies human wants and provides utility, for example, to a consumer making a purchase. A common distinction is made between 'goods' that are tangible property (also called goods) and services, which are non-physical. Commodities may be used as a synonym for economic goods but often refer to marketable raw materials and primary products.
Hong	The Hongs were major business houses in Canton, China and later Hong Kong with significant influence on patterns of consumerism, trade, manufacturing and other key areas of the economy. They were originally led by Howqua as head of the cohong.
Index	In economics and finance, an index is a statistical measure of changes in a representative group of individual data points. These data may be derived from any number of sources, including company performance, prices, productivity, and employment. Economic indices (index, plural) track economic health from different perspectives.
Exit	Exit, in economics, means opting out of future transactions.
Incentive	An incentive is something that motivates an individual to perform an action.

11. Perfect Competition,

CHAPTER HIGHLIGHTS & NOTES: KEY TERMS, PEOPLE, PLACES, CONCEPTS

	The study of incentive structures is central to the study of all economic activities (both in terms of individual decision-making and in terms of co-operation and competition within a larger institutional structure). Economic analysis, then, of the differences between societies (and between different organizations within a society) largely amounts to characterizing the differences in incentive structures faced by individuals involved in these collective efforts.
Income	Income is the consumption and savings opportunity gained by an entity within a specified timeframe, which is generally expressed in monetary terms. However, for households and individuals, 'income is the sum of all the wages, salaries, profits, interests payments, rents and other forms of earnings received... in a given period of time.' In the field of public economics, the term may refer to the accumulation of both monetary and non-monetary consumption ability, with the former (monetary) being used as a proxy for total income.
Technological change	Technological change is a term that is used to describe the overall process of invention, innovation and diffusion of technology or processes. The term is synonymous with technological development, technological achievement, and technological progress. In essence TC is the invention of a technology (or a process), the continuous process of improving a technology (in which it often becomes cheaper) and its diffusion throughout industry or society.
Competitive Market	In economic theory, perfect competition describes markets such that no participants are large enough to have the market power to set the price of a homogeneous product. Because the conditions for perfect competition are strict, there are few if any perfectly competitive markets. Still, buyers and sellers in some auction-type markets, say for commodities (especially decentralised digital commodities such as Bitcoin) or some financial assets, may approximate the concept.
Circular flow	In economics, the terms circular flow of income or circular flow refer to a simple economic model which describes the reciprocal circulation of income between producers and consumers. In the circular flow model, the inter-dependent entities of producer and consumer are referred to as 'firms' and 'households' respectively and provide each other with factors in order to facilitate the flow of income. Firms provide consumers with goods and services in exchange for consumer expenditure and 'factors of production' from households.
Efficiency	The relative efficiency of two procedures is the ratio of their efficiencies, although often this term is used where the comparison is made between a given procedure and a notional 'best possible' procedure. The efficiencies and the relative efficiency of two procedures theoretically depend on the sample size available for the given procedure, but it is often possible to use the asymptotic relative efficiency as the principal comparison measure. Efficiencies are often defined using the variance or mean square error as the measure of desirability.

11. Perfect Competition,

CHAPTER HIGHLIGHTS & NOTES: KEY TERMS, PEOPLE, PLACES, CONCEPTS

Factor	A factor, Latin for 'doer, maker', is a mercantile fiduciary who receives and sells goods on commission (called factorage), transacting business in his own name and not disclosing his principal, and historically with his seat at a factory (trading post). A factor differs from a commission merchant in that a factor takes possession of goods (or documents of title representing goods) on consignment, whereas a commission merchant sells goods not in his possession on the basis of samples. Most modern factor business is in the textile field, but factors are also used to a great extent in the shoe, furniture, hardware, and other industries, and the trade areas in which factors operate have increased.
Competition	In economics, competition is the rivalry among sellers trying to achieve such goals as increasing profits, market share, and sales volume by varying the elements of the marketing mix: price, product, distribution, and promotion. Merriam-Webster defines competition in business as 'the effort of two or more parties acting independently to secure the business of a third party by offering the most favorable terms.' It was described by Adam Smith in The Wealth of Nations (1776) and later economists as allocating productive resources to their most highly-valued uses and encouraging efficiency. Smith and other classical economists before Cournot were referring to price and non-price rivalry among producers to sell their goods on best terms by bidding of buyers, not necessarily to a large number of sellers nor to a market in final equilibrium.
Consumer	A consumer is a person or group of people, such as a household, who are the final users of products or services. The consumer's use is final in the sense that the product is usually not improved by the use.
Production	Production is a process of combining various material inputs and immaterial inputs in order to make something for consumption (the output). It is the act of creating output, a good or service which has value and contributes to the utility of individuals. Economic well-being is created in a production process, meaning all economic activities that aim directly or indirectly to satisfy human needs.

11. Perfect Competition,

CHAPTER QUIZ: KEY TERMS, PEOPLE, PLACES, CONCEPTS

1. In economics and finance, an _____ is a statistical measure of changes in a representative group of individual data points. These data may be derived from any number of sources, including company performance, prices, productivity, and employment. Economic indices (_____, plural) track economic health from different perspectives.

    a. Bayesian vector autoregression
    b. Bootstrapping
    c. Index
    d. Chow test

2. _____ is the total receipts of a firm from the sale of any given quantity of a product.

    It can be calculated as the selling price of the firm's product times the quantity sold, i.e. _____ = price × quantity, or letting TR be the _____ function: $TR(Q) = P(Q) \times Q$

    where Q is the quantity of output sold, and P(Q) is the inverse demand function (the demand function solved out for price in terms of quantity demanded).

    a. Base period
    b. Benefit incidence
    c. Total revenue
    d. Bond

3. A _____ is one of the many varieties of systems, institutions, procedures, social relations and infrastructures whereby parties engage in exchange. While parties may exchange goods and services by barter, most _____s rely on sellers offering their goods or services (including labor) in exchange for money from buyers. It can be said that a _____ is the process by which the prices of goods and services are established.

    a. Contract farming
    b. Convertible husbandry
    c. Corn exchange
    d. Market

4. A _____ (from Greek monos μ???? + polein p??e?? (to sell)) exists when a specific person or enterprise is the only supplier of a particular commodity (this contrasts with a monopsony which relates to a single entity's control of a market to purchase a good or service, and with oligopoly which consists of a few entities dominating an industry). _____(ies) are thus characterized by a lack of economic competition to produce the good or service and a lack of viable substitute goods. The verb 'monopolize' refers to the process by which a company gains the ability to raise prices or exclude competitors.

    a. Contract farming
    b. Convertible husbandry
    c. Corn exchange
    d. Monopoly

11. Perfect Competition,

CHAPTER QUIZ: KEY TERMS, PEOPLE, PLACES, CONCEPTS

5. A _____, Latin for 'doer, maker', is a mercantile fiduciary who receives and sells goods on commission (called factorage), transacting business in his own name and not disclosing his principal, and historically with his seat at a factory (trading post). A _____ differs from a commission merchant in that a _____ takes possession of goods (or documents of title representing goods) on consignment, whereas a commission merchant sells goods not in his possession on the basis of samples. Most modern _____ business is in the textile field, but _____s are also used to a great extent in the shoe, furniture, hardware, and other industries, and the trade areas in which _____s operate have increased.

   a. Factor
   b. Beaver
   c. Boat Encampment
   d. California Fur Rush

ANSWER KEY
11. Perfect Competition,

1. c
2. c
3. d
4. d
5. a

You can take the complete Online Interactive Chapter Practice Test

for 11. Perfect Competition,
on all key terms, persons, places, and concepts.

No Additional Costs

http://www.Cram101.com

Register, send an email request to Travis.Reese@Cram101.com to get your user Id and password.

Include your customer order number, and ISBN number from your studyguide Retailer.

12. Monopoly,

CHAPTER OUTLINE: KEY TERMS, PEOPLE, PLACES, CONCEPTS

	Barriers to entry
	Monopoly
	Natural monopoly
	Natural resource
	Ownership
	Resource
	Copyright law
	Patent
	Marginal revenue
	Total revenue
	Demand
	Index
	Price
	Elasticity
	Cost-push inflation
	Marginal cost
	Total cost
	Output
	Substitution bias
	Business cycle
	Economic profit

12. Monopoly,

CHAPTER OUTLINE: KEY TERMS, PEOPLE, PLACES, CONCEPTS

| Incentive
| Competition
| Deadweight loss
| Industrial Revolution
| Circular flow
| Factor
| Production
| Consumer
| Consumer surplus
| Price discrimination
| Airline
| Efficiency
| Rate
| Average cost
| Average cost pricing
| Fixed cost
| Google
| Cost
| Monopoly price
| Facing

12. Monopoly,

CHAPTER HIGHLIGHTS & NOTES: KEY TERMS, PEOPLE, PLACES, CONCEPTS

Barriers to entry	In theories of competition in economics, barriers to entry, also known as barrier to entry, are obstacles that make it difficult to enter a given market. The term can refer to hindrances a firm faces in trying to enter a market or industry--such as government regulation and patents, or a large, established firm taking advantage of economies of scale--or those an individual faces in trying to gain entrance to a profession--such as education or licensing requirements. Because barriers to entry protect incumbent firms and restrict competition in a market, they can contribute to distortionary prices.
Monopoly	A monopoly (from Greek monos μ???? + polein p??e?? (to sell)) exists when a specific person or enterprise is the only supplier of a particular commodity (this contrasts with a monopsony which relates to a single entity's control of a market to purchase a good or service, and with oligopoly which consists of a few entities dominating an industry). Monopolies are thus characterized by a lack of economic competition to produce the good or service and a lack of viable substitute goods. The verb 'monopolize' refers to the process by which a company gains the ability to raise prices or exclude competitors.
Natural monopoly	A monopoly is a firm which is the only one producing and selling a particular product. A natural monopoly is a monopoly in an industry in which it is most efficient (involving the lowest long-run average cost) for production to be concentrated in a single firm. This market situation gives the largest supplier in an industry, often the first supplier in a market, an overwhelming cost advantage over other actual and potential competitors, so a natural monopoly situation generally leads to an actual monopoly.
Natural resource	Natural resources are resources that exist without actions of humankind. This includes all valued characteristics such as magnetic, gravitational, and electrical properties and forces. On earth it includes; sunlight, atmosphere, water, land, air (includes all minerals) along with all vegetation and animal life that naturally subsists upon or within the heretofore identified characteristics and substances.
Ownership	Ownership of property may be private, collective, or common and the property may be objects, land/real estate, or intellectual property. Determining ownership in law involves determining who has certain rights and duties over the property. These rights and duties, sometimes called a 'bundle of rights', can be separated and held by different parties.
Resource	A resource is a source or supply from which benefit is produced. Typically resources are materials, services, staff, or other assets that are transformed to produce benefit and in the process may be consumed or made unavailable. Benefits of resource utilization may include increased wealth, meeting needs or wants, proper functioning of a system, or enhanced well being.
Copyright law	Copyright is a legal right created by the law of a country that grants the creator of an original work exclusive rights for its use and distribution. This is usually only for a limited time.

12. Monopoly,

CHAPTER HIGHLIGHTS & NOTES: KEY TERMS, PEOPLE, PLACES, CONCEPTS

Patent	A patent is a set of exclusive rights granted by a sovereign state to an inventor or assignee for a limited period of time in exchange for detailed public disclosure of an invention. An invention is a solution to a specific technological problem and is a product or a process. Patents are a form of intellectual property.
Marginal revenue	In microeconomics, marginal revenue is the additional revenue that will be generated by increasing product sales by 1 unit. It can also be described as the unit revenue the last item sold has generated for the firm. In a perfectly competitive market, the additional revenue generated by selling an additional unit of a good is equal to the price the firm is able to charge the buyer of the good.
Total revenue	Total revenue is the total receipts of a firm from the sale of any given quantity of a product. It can be calculated as the selling price of the firm's product times the quantity sold, i.e. total revenue = price × quantity, or letting TR be the total revenue function: $$TR(Q) = P(Q) \times Q$$ where Q is the quantity of output sold, and P(Q) is the inverse demand function (the demand function solved out for price in terms of quantity demanded).
Demand	In economics, demand for a good or service is an entire listing of the quantity of the good or service that a market would choose to buy, for every possible market price of the good or service. (Note: This distinguishes 'demand' from 'quantity demanded', where demand is a listing or graphing of quantity demanded at each possible price. In contrast to demand, quantity demanded is the exact quantity demanded at a certain price.
Index	In economics and finance, an index is a statistical measure of changes in a representative group of individual data points. These data may be derived from any number of sources, including company performance, prices, productivity, and employment. Economic indices (index, plural) track economic health from different perspectives.
Price	In ordinary usage, price is the quantity of payment or compensation given by one party to another in return for goods or services. In modern economies, prices are generally expressed in units of some form of currency. (For commodities, they are expressed as currency per unit weight of the commodity, e.g. euros per kilogram).
Elasticity	In economics, elasticity is the measurement of how responsive an economic variable is to a change in another. For example:•'If I lower the price of my product, how much more will I sell?'•'If I raise the price of one good, how will that affect sales of this other good?'•'If we learn that a resource is becoming scarce, will people scramble to acquire it?'

12. Monopoly,

CHAPTER HIGHLIGHTS & NOTES: KEY TERMS, PEOPLE, PLACES, CONCEPTS

	An elastic variable (or elasticity value greater than 1) is one which responds more than proportionally to changes in other variables. In contrast, an inelastic variable (or elasticity value less than 1) is one which changes less than proportionally in response to changes in other variables.
Cost-push inflation	Cost-push inflation is an alleged type of inflation caused by substantial increases in the cost of important goods or services where no suitable alternative is available. A situation that has been often cited of this was the oil crisis of the 1970s, which some economists see as a major cause of the inflation experienced in the Western world in that decade. It is argued that this inflation resulted from increases in the cost of petroleum imposed by the member states of OPEC. Since petroleum is so important to industrialised economies, a large increase in its price can lead to the increase in the price of most products, raising the inflation rate.
Marginal cost	In economics and finance, marginal cost is the change in the total cost that arises when the quantity produced has an increment by unit. That is, it is the cost of producing one more unit of a good. In general terms, marginal cost at each level of production includes any additional costs required to produce the next unit.
Total cost	In economics, and cost accounting, total cost describes the total economic cost of production and is made up of variable costs, which vary according to the quantity of a good produced and include inputs such as labor and raw materials, plus fixed costs, which are independent of the quantity of a good produced and include inputs (capital) that cannot be varied in the short term, such as buildings and machinery. Total cost in economics includes the total opportunity cost of each factor of production as part of its fixed or variable costs. The rate at which total cost changes as the amount produced changes is called marginal cost.
Output	Output in economics is the 'quantity of goods or services produced in a given time period, by a firm, industry, or country,' whether consumed or used for further production. The concept of national output is absolutely essential in the field of macroeconomics. It is national output that makes a country rich, not large amounts of money.
Substitution bias	Substitution bias describes a bias in economics index numbers arising from tendency to purchase inexpensive substitutes for expensive items when prices change. Substitution bias occurs when two or more items experience a change of price relative to each other. Consumers will consume more of the now comparatively inexpensive good and less of the now relatively more expensive good.

12. Monopoly,

CHAPTER HIGHLIGHTS & NOTES: KEY TERMS, PEOPLE, PLACES, CONCEPTS

Business cycle	The term business cycle refers to economy-wide fluctuations in production, trade and economic activity in general over several months or years in an economy organized on free-enterprise principles.
	The business cycle is the upward and downward movements of levels of GDP (gross domestic product) and refers to the period of expansions and contractions in the level of economic activities (business fluctuations) around its long-term growth trend.
	These fluctuations occur around a long-term growth trend, and typically involve shifts over time between periods of relatively rapid economic growth (an expansion or boom), and periods of relative stagnation or decline (a contraction or recession).
Economic profit	In neoclassical microeconomic theory, the term profit has two related but distinct meanings. Economic profit is similar to accounting profit but smaller because it reflects the total opportunity costs (both explicit and implicit) of a venture to an investor. Normal profit refers to a situation in which the economic profit is zero.
Incentive	An incentive is something that motivates an individual to perform an action. The study of incentive structures is central to the study of all economic activities (both in terms of individual decision-making and in terms of co-operation and competition within a larger institutional structure). Economic analysis, then, of the differences between societies (and between different organizations within a society) largely amounts to characterizing the differences in incentive structures faced by individuals involved in these collective efforts.
Competition	In economics, competition is the rivalry among sellers trying to achieve such goals as increasing profits, market share, and sales volume by varying the elements of the marketing mix: price, product, distribution, and promotion. Merriam-Webster defines competition in business as 'the effort of two or more parties acting independently to secure the business of a third party by offering the most favorable terms.' It was described by Adam Smith in The Wealth of Nations (1776) and later economists as allocating productive resources to their most highly-valued uses and encouraging efficiency. Smith and other classical economists before Cournot were referring to price and non-price rivalry among producers to sell their goods on best terms by bidding of buyers, not necessarily to a large number of sellers nor to a market in final equilibrium.
Deadweight loss	In economics, a deadweight loss is a loss of economic efficiency that can occur when equilibrium for a good or service is not Pareto optimal.
	Causes of deadweight loss can include monopoly pricing (in the case of artificial scarcity), externalities, taxes or subsidies, and binding price ceilings or floors (including minimum wages). The term deadweight loss may also be referred to as the 'excess burden' of monopoly or taxation.

12. Monopoly,

CHAPTER HIGHLIGHTS & NOTES: KEY TERMS, PEOPLE, PLACES, CONCEPTS

Industrial Revolution	The Industrial Revolution was the transition to new manufacturing processes in the period from about 1760 to sometime between 1820 and 1840. This transition included going from hand production methods to machines, new chemical manufacturing and iron production processes, improved efficiency of water power, the increasing use of steam power and the development of machine tools. It also included the change from wood and other bio-fuels to coal. Textiles were the dominant industry of the Industrial Revolution in terms of employment, value of output and capital invested.
Circular flow	In economics, the terms circular flow of income or circular flow refer to a simple economic model which describes the reciprocal circulation of income between producers and consumers. In the circular flow model, the inter-dependent entities of producer and consumer are referred to as 'firms' and 'households' respectively and provide each other with factors in order to facilitate the flow of income. Firms provide consumers with goods and services in exchange for consumer expenditure and 'factors of production' from households.
Factor	A factor, Latin for 'doer, maker', is a mercantile fiduciary who receives and sells goods on commission (called factorage), transacting business in his own name and not disclosing his principal, and historically with his seat at a factory (trading post). A factor differs from a commission merchant in that a factor takes possession of goods (or documents of title representing goods) on consignment, whereas a commission merchant sells goods not in his possession on the basis of samples. Most modern factor business is in the textile field, but factors are also used to a great extent in the shoe, furniture, hardware, and other industries, and the trade areas in which factors operate have increased.
Production	Production is a process of combining various material inputs and immaterial inputs in order to make something for consumption (the output). It is the act of creating output, a good or service which has value and contributes to the utility of individuals. Economic well-being is created in a production process, meaning all economic activities that aim directly or indirectly to satisfy human needs.
Consumer	A consumer is a person or group of people, such as a household, who are the final users of products or services. The consumer's use is final in the sense that the product is usually not improved by the use.
Consumer surplus	In mainstream economics, economic surplus (also known as total welfare or Marshallian surplus) refers to two related quantities. Consumer surplus or consumers' surplus is the monetary gain obtained by consumers because they are able to purchase a product for a price that is less than the highest price that they would be willing to pay. Producer surplus or producers' surplus is the amount that producers benefit by selling at a market price that is higher than the least that they would be willing to sell for.

12. Monopoly,

CHAPTER HIGHLIGHTS & NOTES: KEY TERMS, PEOPLE, PLACES, CONCEPTS

Price discrimination	Price discrimination or price differentiation is a pricing strategy where identical or largely similar goods or services are transacted at different prices by the same provider in different markets or territories. Price differentiation is distinguished from product differentiation by the more substantial difference in production cost for the differently priced products involved in the latter strategy. Price differentiation essentially relies on the variation in the customers' willingness to pay.
Airline	An airline is a company that provides air transport services for traveling passengers and freight. Airlines lease or own their aircraft with which to supply these services and may form partnerships or alliances with other airlines for mutual benefit. Generally, airline companies are recognized with an air operating certificate or license issued by a governmental aviation body.
Efficiency	The relative efficiency of two procedures is the ratio of their efficiencies, although often this term is used where the comparison is made between a given procedure and a notional 'best possible' procedure. The efficiencies and the relative efficiency of two procedures theoretically depend on the sample size available for the given procedure, but it is often possible to use the asymptotic relative efficiency as the principal comparison measure. Efficiencies are often defined using the variance or mean square error as the measure of desirability.
Rate	In mathematics, a rate is a ratio between two measurements with different units. If the unit or quantity in respect of which something is changing is not specified, usually the rate is per unit time. However, a rate of change can be specified per unit time, or per unit of length or mass or another quantity.
Average cost	In economics, average cost or unit cost is equal to total cost divided by the number of goods produced . It is also equal to the sum of average variable costs (total variable costs divided by Q) plus average fixed costs (total fixed costs divided by Q). Average costs may be dependent on the time period considered (increasing production may be expensive or impossible in the short term, for example).
Average cost pricing	Average cost pricing is one of the ways government regulate a monopoly market. Monopolists tend to produce less than the optimal quantity pushing the prices up. Government may use average cost pricing as a tool to regulate prices monopolists may charge.
Fixed cost	In economics, fixed costs, indirect costs or overheads are business expenses that are not dependent on the level of goods or services produced by the business. They tend to be time-related, such as salaries or rents being paid per month, and are often referred to as overhead costs. This is in contrast to variable costs, which are volume-related (and are paid per quantity produced).

12. Monopoly,

CHAPTER HIGHLIGHTS & NOTES: KEY TERMS, PEOPLE, PLACES, CONCEPTS

Google	Google is an American multinational corporation specializing in Internet-related services and products. These include search, cloud computing, software, and online advertising technologies. Most of its profits are derived from AdWords.
Cost	In production, research, retail, and accounting, a cost is the value of money that has been used up to produce something, and hence is not available for use anymore. In business, the cost may be one of acquisition, in which case the amount of money expended to acquire it is counted as cost. In this case, money is the input that is gone in order to acquire the thing.
Monopoly price	A monopoly price is set by a monopoly. A monopoly occurs when a firm is the only firm in an industry producing the product, such that the monopoly faces no competition. A monopoly has absolute market power, and thereby can set a monopoly price that will be above the firm's marginal (economic) cost, which is the change in total (economic) cost due to one additional unit produced.
Facing	Facing is a common tool in the retail industry to create the look of a perfectly stocked store (even when it is not) by pulling all of the products on a display or shelf to the front, as well as down stacking all the canned and stacked items. It is also done to keep the store appearing neat and organized. The workers who perform this task normally have jobs doing other things in the store such as customer service, stocking shelves, daytime cleaning, bagging and carry outs (in grocery stores), etc.

CHAPTER QUIZ: KEY TERMS, PEOPLE, PLACES, CONCEPTS

1. In theories of competition in economics, _____, also known as barrier to entry, are obstacles that make it difficult to enter a given market. The term can refer to hindrances a firm faces in trying to enter a market or industry--such as government regulation and patents, or a large, established firm taking advantage of economies of scale--or those an individual faces in trying to gain entrance to a profession--such as education or licensing requirements.

   Because _____ protect incumbent firms and restrict competition in a market, they can contribute to distortionary prices.

   a. Fuel protests in the United Kingdom
   b. Barriers to entry
   c. Freikorps Lichtschlag
   d. Freikorps Oberland

2. . _____ is the total receipts of a firm from the sale of any given quantity of a product.

   It can be calculated as the selling price of the firm's product times the quantity sold, i.e.

12. Monopoly,

CHAPTER QUIZ: KEY TERMS, PEOPLE, PLACES, CONCEPTS

_____ = price × quantity, or letting TR be the _____ function: $TR(Q) = P(Q) \times Q$

where Q is the quantity of output sold, and P(Q) is the inverse demand function (the demand function solved out for price in terms of quantity demanded).

a. Total revenue
b. Benefit incidence
c. Blanket order
d. Bond

3. In microeconomics, _____ is the additional revenue that will be generated by increasing product sales by 1 unit. It can also be described as the unit revenue the last item sold has generated for the firm. In a perfectly competitive market, the additional revenue generated by selling an additional unit of a good is equal to the price the firm is able to charge the buyer of the good.

a. Benefit principle
b. Marginal revenue
c. Club good
d. Conjectural variation

4. A _____ is a set of exclusive rights granted by a sovereign state to an inventor or assignee for a limited period of time in exchange for detailed public disclosure of an invention. An invention is a solution to a specific technological problem and is a product or a process. _____s are a form of intellectual property.

a. Common Agricultural Policy
b. Commodity Credit Corporation
c. Patent
d. Contract farming

5. A _____, Latin for 'doer, maker', is a mercantile fiduciary who receives and sells goods on commission (called factorage), transacting business in his own name and not disclosing his principal, and historically with his seat at a factory (trading post). A _____ differs from a commission merchant in that a _____ takes possession of goods (or documents of title representing goods) on consignment, whereas a commission merchant sells goods not in his possession on the basis of samples. Most modern _____ business is in the textile field, but _____s are also used to a great extent in the shoe, furniture, hardware, and other industries, and the trade areas in which _____s operate have increased.

a. Bateau
b. Beaver
c. Boat Encampment
d. Factor

ANSWER KEY
12. Monopoly,

1. b
2. a
3. b
4. c
5. d

You can take the complete Online Interactive Chapter Practice Test

for 12. Monopoly,
on all key terms, persons, places, and concepts.

No Additional Costs

http://www.Cram101.com

Register, send an email request to Travis.Reese@Cram101.com to get your user Id and password.

Include your customer order number, and ISBN number from your studyguide Retailer.

13. Monopolistic Competition and Oligopoly,

CHAPTER OUTLINE: KEY TERMS, PEOPLE, PLACES, CONCEPTS

	Business cycle
	Collusion
	Market
	Monopolistic competition
	Product differentiation
	Purchasing power
	Competition law
	Price
	Product
	Quality
	Theory
	Bias
	Substitution bias
	Competition
	Economy
	Economic profit
	Long
	Long run
	Index
	Perfect competition
	Electronic Arts

13. Monopolistic Competition and Oligopoly,

CHAPTER OUTLINE: KEY TERMS, PEOPLE, PLACES, CONCEPTS

- _____ Marginal cost
- _____ Circular flow
- _____ Innovation
- _____ Product innovation
- _____ Samsung
- _____ Expenditure
- _____ Total cost
- _____ Cost
- _____ Cost-push inflation
- _____ Demand
- _____ Efficiency
- _____ Selling
- _____ Cartel
- _____ Duopoly
- _____ Airbus
- _____ Outcome
- _____ Game theory
- _____ Nash equilibrium
- _____ Matrix
- _____ Advertising
- _____ Repeated game

13. Monopolistic Competition and Oligopoly,
CHAPTER OUTLINE: KEY TERMS, PEOPLE, PLACES, CONCEPTS

	Consumer
	Google
	Oligopoly

CHAPTER HIGHLIGHTS & NOTES: KEY TERMS, PEOPLE, PLACES, CONCEPTS

Business cycle	The term business cycle refers to economy-wide fluctuations in production, trade and economic activity in general over several months or years in an economy organized on free-enterprise principles. The business cycle is the upward and downward movements of levels of GDP (gross domestic product) and refers to the period of expansions and contractions in the level of economic activities (business fluctuations) around its long-term growth trend. These fluctuations occur around a long-term growth trend, and typically involve shifts over time between periods of relatively rapid economic growth (an expansion or boom), and periods of relative stagnation or decline (a contraction or recession).
Collusion	Collusion is an agreement between two or more parties, sometimes illegal and therefore secretive, to limit open competition by deceiving, misleading, or defrauding others of their legal rights, or to obtain an objective forbidden by law typically by defrauding or gaining an unfair advantage. It is an agreement among firms or individuals to divide a market, set prices, limit production or limit opportunities. It can involve 'wage fixing, kickbacks, or misrepresenting the independence of the relationship between the colluding parties'.
Market	A market is one of the many varieties of systems, institutions, procedures, social relations and infrastructures whereby parties engage in exchange. While parties may exchange goods and services by barter, most markets rely on sellers offering their goods or services (including labor) in exchange for money from buyers. It can be said that a market is the process by which the prices of goods and services are established.
Monopolistic competition	Monopolistic competition is a type of imperfect competition such that many producers sell products that are differentiated from one another and hence are not perfect substitutes.

13. Monopolistic Competition and Oligopoly,

CHAPTER HIGHLIGHTS & NOTES: KEY TERMS, PEOPLE, PLACES, CONCEPTS

	In monopolistic competition, a firm takes the prices charged by its rivals as given and ignores the impact of its own prices on the prices of other firms. In the presence of coercive government, monopolistic competition will fall into government-granted monopoly.
Product differentiation	In economics and marketing, product differentiation is the process of distinguishing a product or service from others, to make it more attractive to a particular target market. This involves differentiating it from competitors' products as well as a firm's own products. The concept was proposed by Edward Chamberlin in his 1933 Theory of Monopolistic Competition.
Purchasing power	Purchasing power is the number of goods or services that can be purchased with a unit of currency. For example, if one had taken one unit of currency to a store in the 1950s, it is probable that it would have been possible to buy a greater number of items than would today, indicating that one would have had a greater purchasing power in the 1950s. Currency can be either a commodity money, like gold or silver, or fiat currency, or free-floating market-valued currency like US dollars.
Competition law	Competition law is law that promotes or seeks to maintain market competition by regulating anti-competitive conduct by companies. Competition law is known as antitrust law in the United States and anti-monopoly law in China and Russia. In previous years it has been known as trade practices law in the United Kingdom and Australia.
Price	In ordinary usage, price is the quantity of payment or compensation given by one party to another in return for goods or services. In modern economies, prices are generally expressed in units of some form of currency. (For commodities, they are expressed as currency per unit weight of the commodity, e.g. euros per kilogram).
Product	In marketing, a product is anything that can be offered to a market that might satisfy a want or need. In retailing, products are called merchandise. In manufacturing, products are bought as raw materials and sold as finished goods.
Quality	Quality in business, engineering and manufacturing has a pragmatic interpretation as the non-inferiority or superiority of something; it is also defined as fitness for purpose. Quality is a perceptual, conditional, and somewhat subjective attribute and may be understood differently by different people. Consumers may focus on the specification quality of a product/service, or how it compares to competitors in the marketplace.
Theory	Theory is a group of ideas meant to explain a certain topic of science, such as a single or collection of fact, event(s), or phenomen(a)(on). Typically, a theory is developed through the use of contemplative and rational forms of abstract and generalized thinking.

13. Monopolistic Competition and Oligopoly,

CHAPTER HIGHLIGHTS & NOTES: KEY TERMS, PEOPLE, PLACES, CONCEPTS

Bias	A statistic is biased if it is calculated in such a way that it is systematically different from the population parameter of interest. The following lists some types of biases, which can overlap. •Selection bias,involves individuals being more likely to be selected for study than others, biasing the sample.
Substitution bias	Substitution bias describes a bias in economics index numbers arising from tendency to purchase inexpensive substitutes for expensive items when prices change. Substitution bias occurs when two or more items experience a change of price relative to each other. Consumers will consume more of the now comparatively inexpensive good and less of the now relatively more expensive good.
Competition	In economics, competition is the rivalry among sellers trying to achieve such goals as increasing profits, market share, and sales volume by varying the elements of the marketing mix: price, product, distribution, and promotion. Merriam-Webster defines competition in business as 'the effort of two or more parties acting independently to secure the business of a third party by offering the most favorable terms.' It was described by Adam Smith in The Wealth of Nations (1776) and later economists as allocating productive resources to their most highly-valued uses and encouraging efficiency. Smith and other classical economists before Cournot were referring to price and non-price rivalry among producers to sell their goods on best terms by bidding of buyers, not necessarily to a large number of sellers nor to a market in final equilibrium.
Economy	An economy or economic system consists of the production, distribution or trade, and consumption of limited goods and services by different agents in a given geographical location. The economic agents can be individuals, businesses, organizations, or governments. Transactions occur when two parties agree to the value or price of the transacted good or service, commonly expressed in a certain currency.
Economic profit	In neoclassical microeconomic theory, the term profit has two related but distinct meanings. Economic profit is similar to accounting profit but smaller because it reflects the total opportunity costs (both explicit and implicit) of a venture to an investor. Normal profit refers to a situation in which the economic profit is zero.
Long	Long/short equity is an investment strategy generally associated with hedge funds, and more recently certain progressive traditional asset managers. It involves buying long equities that are expected to increase in value and selling short equities that are expected to decrease in value. This is different from the risk reversal strategies where investors will simultaneously buy a call option and sell a put option to simulate being long in a stock.
Long run	In microeconomics, the long run is the conceptual time period in which there are no fixed factors of production as to changing the output level by changing the capital stock or by entering or leaving an industry.

13. Monopolistic Competition and Oligopoly,

CHAPTER HIGHLIGHTS & NOTES: KEY TERMS, PEOPLE, PLACES, CONCEPTS

	The long run contrasts with the short run, in which some factors are variable and others are fixed, constraining entry or exit from an industry. In macroeconomics, the long run is the period when the general price level, contractual wage rates, and expectations adjust fully to the state of the economy, in contrast to the short run when these variables may not fully adjust.
Index	In economics and finance, an index is a statistical measure of changes in a representative group of individual data points. These data may be derived from any number of sources, including company performance, prices, productivity, and employment. Economic indices (index, plural) track economic health from different perspectives.
Perfect competition	In economic theory, perfect competition describes markets such that no participants are large enough to have the market power to set the price of a homogeneous product. Because the conditions for perfect competition are strict, there are few if any perfectly competitive markets. Still, buyers and sellers in some auction-type markets, say for commodities or some financial assets, may approximate the concept.
Electronic Arts	Electronic Arts, Inc. (EA) is an American developer, marketer, publisher and distributor of video games headquartered in Redwood City, California, USA. Founded and incorporated on May 28, 1982 by Trip Hawkins, the company was a pioneer of the early home computer games industry and was notable for promoting the designers and programmers responsible for its games. In 2011 Electronic Arts was the world's third-largest gaming company by revenue after Nintendo and Activision Blizzard.
Marginal cost	In economics and finance, marginal cost is the change in the total cost that arises when the quantity produced has an increment by unit. That is, it is the cost of producing one more unit of a good. In general terms, marginal cost at each level of production includes any additional costs required to produce the next unit.
Circular flow	In economics, the terms circular flow of income or circular flow refer to a simple economic model which describes the reciprocal circulation of income between producers and consumers. In the circular flow model, the inter-dependent entities of producer and consumer are referred to as 'firms' and 'households' respectively and provide each other with factors in order to facilitate the flow of income. Firms provide consumers with goods and services in exchange for consumer expenditure and 'factors of production' from households.
Innovation	In time series analysis -- as conducted in statistics, signal processing, and many other fields -- the innovation is the difference between the observed value of a variable at time t and the optimal forecast of that value based on information available prior to time t. If the forecasting method is working correctly successive innovations are uncorrelated with each other, i.e., constitute a white noise time series. Thus it can be said that the innovation time series is obtained from the measurement time series by a process of 'whitening', or removing the predictable component.

13. Monopolistic Competition and Oligopoly,

CHAPTER HIGHLIGHTS & NOTES: KEY TERMS, PEOPLE, PLACES, CONCEPTS

Product innovation	Product innovation is the creation and subsequent introduction of a good or service that is either new, or improved on previous goods or services. This is broader than the normally accepted definition of innovation to include invention of new products which, in this context, are still considered innovative.
Samsung	Samsung Group is a South Korean multinational conglomerate company headquartered in Samsung Town, Seoul. It comprises numerous subsidiaries and affiliated businesses, most of them united under the Samsung brand, and is the largest South Korean chaebol (business conglomerate). Samsung was founded by Lee Byung-chul in 1938 as a trading company.
Expenditure	In common usage, an expense or expenditure is an outflow of money to another person or group to pay for an item or service, or for a category of costs. For a tenant, rent is an expense. For students or parents, tuition is an expense.
Total cost	In economics, and cost accounting, total cost describes the total economic cost of production and is made up of variable costs, which vary according to the quantity of a good produced and include inputs such as labor and raw materials, plus fixed costs, which are independent of the quantity of a good produced and include inputs (capital) that cannot be varied in the short term, such as buildings and machinery. Total cost in economics includes the total opportunity cost of each factor of production as part of its fixed or variable costs. The rate at which total cost changes as the amount produced changes is called marginal cost.
Cost	In production, research, retail, and accounting, a cost is the value of money that has been used up to produce something, and hence is not available for use anymore. In business, the cost may be one of acquisition, in which case the amount of money expended to acquire it is counted as cost. In this case, money is the input that is gone in order to acquire the thing.
Cost-push inflation	Cost-push inflation is an alleged type of inflation caused by substantial increases in the cost of important goods or services where no suitable alternative is available. A situation that has been often cited of this was the oil crisis of the 1970s, which some economists see as a major cause of the inflation experienced in the Western world in that decade. It is argued that this inflation resulted from increases in the cost of petroleum imposed by the member states of OPEC. Since petroleum is so important to industrialised economies, a large increase in its price can lead to the increase in the price of most products, raising the inflation rate.
Demand	In economics, demand for a good or service is an entire listing of the quantity of the good or service that a market would choose to buy, for every possible market price of the good or service. (Note: This distinguishes 'demand' from 'quantity demanded', where demand is a listing or graphing of quantity demanded at each possible price.

13. Monopolistic Competition and Oligopoly,

CHAPTER HIGHLIGHTS & NOTES: KEY TERMS, PEOPLE, PLACES, CONCEPTS

Efficiency	The relative efficiency of two procedures is the ratio of their efficiencies, although often this term is used where the comparison is made between a given procedure and a notional 'best possible' procedure. The efficiencies and the relative efficiency of two procedures theoretically depend on the sample size available for the given procedure, but it is often possible to use the asymptotic relative efficiency as the principal comparison measure. Efficiencies are often defined using the variance or mean square error as the measure of desirability.
Selling	Selling is offering to exchange an item of value for a different item. The original item of value being offered may be either tangible or intangible. The second item, usually money, is most often seen by the seller as being of equal or greater value than that being offered for sale.
Cartel	A cartel is a formal 'agreement' among competing firms. It is a formal organization of producers and manufacturers that agree to fix prices, marketing, and production. Cartels usually occur in an oligopolistic industry, where the number of sellers is small (usually because barriers to entry, most notably startup costs, are high) and the products being traded are usually commodities.
Duopoly	A duopoly is a situation in television and radio broadcasting in which two or more stations in the same city or community share common ownership.
Airbus	Airbus SAS is an aircraft manufacturing division of Airbus Group (formerly European Aeronautic Defence and Space Company). Based in Blagnac, France, a suburb of Toulouse, with production and manufacturing facilities mainly in France, Germany, Spain and the United Kingdom, the company produced 626 airliners in 2013. Airbus began as a consortium of aerospace manufacturers, Airbus Industrie.
Outcome	In game theory, an outcome is a set of moves or strategies taken by the players, or it is their payoffs resulting from the actions or strategies taken by all players. The two are complementary in that, given knowledge of the set of strategies of all players, the final state of the game is known, as are any relevant payoffs. In a game where chance or a random event is involved, the outcome is not known from only the set of strategies, but is only realized when the random event(s) are realized.
Game theory	Game theory is a study of strategic decision making. Specifically, it is 'the study of mathematical models of conflict and cooperation between intelligent rational decision-makers'. An alternative term suggested 'as a more descriptive name for the discipline' is interactive decision theory.
Nash equilibrium	In game theory, the Nash equilibrium is a solution concept of a non-cooperative game involving two or more players, in which each player is assumed to know the equilibrium strategies of the other players, and no player has anything to gain by changing only their own strategy.

13. Monopolistic Competition and Oligopoly,
CHAPTER HIGHLIGHTS & NOTES: KEY TERMS, PEOPLE, PLACES, CONCEPTS

	If each player has chosen a strategy and no player can benefit by changing strategies while the other players keep theirs unchanged, then the current set of strategy choices and the corresponding payoffs constitute a Nash equilibrium.
	Stated simply, Amy and Wili are in Nash equilibrium if Amy is making the best decision she can, taking into account Wili's decision, and Wili is making the best decision he can, taking into account Amy's decision.
Matrix	In numismatics, a matrix is an intermediate mould used in the process of manufacturing coins.
	A matrix has its design in the same sense as a die. The design is engraved convex into the matrix, which is used to create punches.
Advertising	Advertising or advertizing in business is a form of marketing communication used to encourage, persuade, or manipulate an audience to take or continue to take some action. Most commonly, the desired result is to drive consumer behavior with respect to a commercial offering, although political and ideological advertising is also common. This type of work belongs to a category called affective labor.
Repeated game	In game theory, a repeated game is an extensive form game which consists in some number of repetitions of some base game (called a stage game). The stage game is usually one of the well-studied 2-person games. It captures the idea that a player will have to take into account the impact of his current action on the future actions of other players; this is sometimes called his reputation.
Consumer	A consumer is a person or group of people, such as a household, who are the final users of products or services. The consumer's use is final in the sense that the product is usually not improved by the use.
Google	Google is an American multinational corporation specializing in Internet-related services and products. These include search, cloud computing, software, and online advertising technologies. Most of its profits are derived from AdWords.
Oligopoly	An oligopoly is a market form in which a market or industry is dominated by a small number of sellers . Oligopolies can result from various forms of collusion which reduce competition and lead to higher prices for consumers.
	With few sellers, each oligopolist is likely to be aware of the actions of the others.

13. Monopolistic Competition and Oligopoly,

CHAPTER QUIZ: KEY TERMS, PEOPLE, PLACES, CONCEPTS

1. _____ is the number of goods or services that can be purchased with a unit of currency. For example, if one had taken one unit of currency to a store in the 1950s, it is probable that it would have been possible to buy a greater number of items than would today, indicating that one would have had a greater _____ in the 1950s. Currency can be either a commodity money, like gold or silver, or fiat currency, or free-floating market-valued currency like US dollars.

    a. Purchasing power
    b. Bilateral descent
    c. Biological determination
    d. Causation

2. _____ is offering to exchange an item of value for a different item. The original item of value being offered may be either tangible or intangible. The second item, usually money, is most often seen by the seller as being of equal or greater value than that being offered for sale.

    a. Selling
    b. Conditional sale
    c. Contract of sale
    d. Contract sales organization

3. A _____ is a situation in television and radio broadcasting in which two or more stations in the same city or community share common ownership.

    a. Concentration of media ownership
    b. Duopoly
    c. Media conglomerate
    d. Media ownership in Australia

4. In game theory, the _____ is a solution concept of a non-cooperative game involving two or more players, in which each player is assumed to know the equilibrium strategies of the other players, and no player has anything to gain by changing only their own strategy. If each player has chosen a strategy and no player can benefit by changing strategies while the other players keep theirs unchanged, then the current set of strategy choices and the corresponding payoffs constitute a _____.

    Stated simply, Amy and Wili are in _____ if Amy is making the best decision she can, taking into account Wili's decision, and Wili is making the best decision he can, taking into account Amy's decision.

    a. Backgammon opening theory
    b. Backward induction
    c. Nash equilibrium
    d. Bayesian efficiency

5. . In microeconomics, the _____ is the conceptual time period in which there are no fixed factors of production as to changing the output level by changing the capital stock or by entering or leaving an industry.

13. Monopolistic Competition and Oligopoly,

CHAPTER QUIZ: KEY TERMS, PEOPLE, PLACES, CONCEPTS

The _____ contrasts with the short run, in which some factors are variable and others are fixed, constraining entry or exit from an industry. In macroeconomics, the _____ is the period when the general price level, contractual wage rates, and expectations adjust fully to the state of the economy, in contrast to the short run when these variables may not fully adjust.

a. Constant elasticity of transformation
b. Cost-of-production theory of value
c. Long run
d. Division of work

ANSWER KEY
13. Monopolistic Competition and Oligopoly,

1. a
2. a
3. b
4. c
5. c

You can take the complete Online Interactive Chapter Practice Test

for 13. Monopolistic Competition and Oligopoly,
on all key terms, persons, places, and concepts.

No Additional Costs

http://www.Cram101.com

Register, send an email request to Travis.Reese@Cram101.com to get your user Id and password.

Include your customer order number, and ISBN number from your studyguide Retailer.

14. GDP: A Measure of Total Production and Income,

CHAPTER OUTLINE: KEY TERMS, PEOPLE, PLACES, CONCEPTS

	Final good
	Gros
	Gross domestic product
	Intermediate good
	Market value
	Good
	Goods and services
	Market
	Service
	Capital good
	Circular flow
	Consumption
	Durable good
	Investment
	Capital
	Economy
	Import
	Export
	Saving
	Expenditure
	Factor

14. GDP: A Measure of Total Production and Income,
CHAPTER OUTLINE: KEY TERMS, PEOPLE, PLACES, CONCEPTS

- _____ Factor cost
- _____ Net export
- _____ Product
- _____ Financial market
- _____ Income
- _____ Bureau of Economic Analysis
- _____ Software
- _____ Interest
- _____ Market price
- _____ Index
- _____ Profit
- _____ Depreciation
- _____ Disposable personal income
- _____ Gross national product
- _____ Production
- _____ Nominal GDP
- _____ Real GDP
- _____ Standard of living
- _____ Value
- _____ Business cycle
- _____ Recession

14. GDP: A Measure of Total Production and Income,

CHAPTER OUTLINE: KEY TERMS, PEOPLE, PLACES, CONCEPTS

	PHASE
	Gift
	Hong
	International Monetary Fund
	Purchasing power
	Purchasing power parity
	Nature
	EDGAR
	Household
	Underground
	Life expectancy
	Social justice
	Price level
	Relative price
	Relative

14. GDP: A Measure of Total Production and Income,

CHAPTER HIGHLIGHTS & NOTES: KEY TERMS, PEOPLE, PLACES, CONCEPTS

Final good	In economics, any commodity which is produced and subsequently consumed by the consumer, to satisfy its current wants or needs, is a consumer good or final good. Consumer goods are goods that are ultimately consumed rather than used in the production of another good. For example, a microwave oven or a bicycle which is sold to a consumer is a final good or consumer good, whereas the components which are sold to be used in those goods are called intermediate goods.
Gros	A gros was a type of silver coinage of France from the time of Saint Louis. There were gros tournois and gros parisis. The gros was sub-divided in half gros and quarter gros.
Gross domestic product	Gross domestic product is the market value of all officially recognized final goods and services produced within a country in a year, or other given period of time. Gross domestic product per capita is often considered an indicator of a country's standard of living. Gross domestic product per capita is not a measure of personal income .
Intermediate good	Intermediate goods or producer goods or semi-finished products are goods used as inputs in the production of other goods, such as partly finished goods. Also, they are goods used in production of final goods. A firm may make and then use intermediate goods, or make and then sell, or buy then use them.
Market value	Market value or OMV is the price at which an asset would trade in a competitive auction setting. Market value is often used interchangeably with open market value, fair value or fair market value, although these terms have distinct definitions in different standards, and may differ in some circumstances.
Good	In economics, a good is a material that satisfies human wants and provides utility, for example, to a consumer making a purchase. A common distinction is made between 'goods' that are tangible property (also called goods) and services, which are non-physical. Commodities may be used as a synonym for economic goods but often refer to marketable raw materials and primary products.
Goods and services	In economics, goods and services are the outcome of human efforts to meet the wants and needs of people. Economic output is divided into physical goods and intangible services. Goods are items that can be seen and touched, such as books, pens, salt, shoes, hats, and folders.
Market	A market is one of the many varieties of systems, institutions, procedures, social relations and infrastructures whereby parties engage in exchange. While parties may exchange goods and services by barter, most markets rely on sellers offering their goods or services (including labor) in exchange for money from buyers. It can be said that a market is the process by which the prices of goods and services are established.
Service	In economics, a service is an intangible commodity. That is, services are an example of intangible economic goods.

14. GDP: A Measure of Total Production and Income,

CHAPTER HIGHLIGHTS & NOTES: KEY TERMS, PEOPLE, PLACES, CONCEPTS

Capital good	A capital good is a durable good that is used in the production of goods or services. Capital goods are one of the three types of producer goods, the other two being land and labor, which are also known collectively as primary factors of production. This classification originated during the classical economic period and has remained the dominant method for classification.
Circular flow	In economics, the terms circular flow of income or circular flow refer to a simple economic model which describes the reciprocal circulation of income between producers and consumers. In the circular flow model, the inter-dependent entities of producer and consumer are referred to as 'firms' and 'households' respectively and provide each other with factors in order to facilitate the flow of income. Firms provide consumers with goods and services in exchange for consumer expenditure and 'factors of production' from households.
Consumption	Consumption is a major concept in economics and is also studied by many other social sciences. Economists are particularly interested in the relationship between consumption and income, and therefore in economics the consumption function plays a major role.

Different schools of economists define production and consumption differently. |
| Durable good | In economics, a durable good or a hard good is a good that does not quickly wear out, or more specifically, one that yields utility over time rather than being completely consumed in one use. Items like bricks could be considered perfectly durable goods, because they should theoretically never wear out. Highly durable goods such as refrigerators, cars, or mobile phones usually continue to be useful for three or more years of use, so durable goods are typically characterized by long periods between successive purchases. |
| Investment | Investment is time, energy, or matter spent in the hope of future benefits. Investment has different meanings in economics and finance.

In economics, investment is the accumulation of newly produced physical entities, such as factories, machinery, houses, and goods inventories. |
| Capital | In economics, capital goods, real capital, or capital assets are already-produced durable goods or any non-financial asset that is used in production of goods or services.

Capital goods are not significantly consumed in the production process though they may depreciate. How a capital good or is maintained or returned to its pre-production state varies with the type of capital involved. |
| Economy | An economy or economic system consists of the production, distribution or trade, and consumption of limited goods and services by different agents in a given geographical location. The economic agents can be individuals, businesses, organizations, or governments. |

14. GDP: A Measure of Total Production and Income,

CHAPTER HIGHLIGHTS & NOTES: KEY TERMS, PEOPLE, PLACES, CONCEPTS

Import	An import is a good brought into a jurisdiction, especially across a national border, from an external source. The purchaser of the exotic good is called an importer. An import in the receiving country is an export from the sending country.
Export	The term export means shipping the goods and services out of the port of a country. The seller of such goods and services is referred to as an 'exporter' who is based in the country of export whereas the overseas based buyer is referred to as an 'importer'. In International Trade, 'exports' refers to selling goods and services produced in the home country to other markets.
Saving	Precautionary savings occurs in response to uncertainty regarding future income. The precautionary motive to delay consumption and save in the current period rises due to the lack of completeness of insurance markets. Accordingly, individuals will not be able to insure against some bad state of the economy in the future.
Expenditure	In common usage, an expense or expenditure is an outflow of money to another person or group to pay for an item or service, or for a category of costs. For a tenant, rent is an expense. For students or parents, tuition is an expense.
Factor	A factor, Latin for 'doer, maker', is a mercantile fiduciary who receives and sells goods on commission (called factorage), transacting business in his own name and not disclosing his principal, and historically with his seat at a factory (trading post). A factor differs from a commission merchant in that a factor takes possession of goods (or documents of title representing goods) on consignment, whereas a commission merchant sells goods not in his possession on the basis of samples. Most modern factor business is in the textile field, but factors are also used to a great extent in the shoe, furniture, hardware, and other industries, and the trade areas in which factors operate have increased.
Factor cost	Factor cost has the following uses in economics:•Factor cost can also refer to the unit cost of a particular factor of production (input in the production process), such as the wage rate or the rental rate of capital.•Factor Cost or Factor Income are the incomes received by the owners of the production (the households) for rendering their factor services to the producers. Corresponding to the real flow of factor services from the households to the producers, there is a money flow from the producers to the households in the form of rent,interest,profit and wages. As a consequences of these flows, there is a production of goods and services in the economy..
Net export	The commercial balance or net exports, is the difference between the monetary value of exports and imports of output in an economy over a certain period, measured in the currency of that economy. It is the relationship between a nation's imports and exports. A positive balance is known as a trade surplus if it consists of exporting more than is imported; a negative balance is referred to as a trade deficit or, informally, a trade gap.

14. GDP: A Measure of Total Production and Income,

CHAPTER HIGHLIGHTS & NOTES: KEY TERMS, PEOPLE, PLACES, CONCEPTS

Product	In marketing, a product is anything that can be offered to a market that might satisfy a want or need. In retailing, products are called merchandise. In manufacturing, products are bought as raw materials and sold as finished goods.
Financial market	A financial market is a market in which people and entities can trade financial securities, commodities, and other fungible items of value at low transaction costs and at prices that reflect supply and demand. Securities include stocks and bonds, and commodities include precious metals or agricultural goods. There are both general markets (where many commodities are traded) and specialized markets (where only one commodity is traded).
Income	Income is the consumption and savings opportunity gained by an entity within a specified timeframe, which is generally expressed in monetary terms. However, for households and individuals, 'income is the sum of all the wages, salaries, profits, interests payments, rents and other forms of earnings received... in a given period of time.' In the field of public economics, the term may refer to the accumulation of both monetary and non-monetary consumption ability, with the former (monetary) being used as a proxy for total income.
Bureau of Economic Analysis	The Bureau of Economic Analysis is an agency in the United States Department of Commerce that provides important economic statistics including the gross domestic product of the United States. BEA is a principal agency of the U.S. Federal Statistical System. Its stated mission is to 'promote a better understanding of the U.S. economy by providing the most timely, relevant, and accurate economic data in an objective and cost-effective manner'.
Software	In development cooperation jargon, 'software' and 'hardware' refer to the different aspects of technology transfer. Whilst the hardware refers to the technology itself, software refers to the skills, knowledge and capacity that need to be built up in order to make the transfer of the technology successful. A third term, 'orgware', is emerging to refer to the capacity building of the different institutional actors involved in the adaptation process of a new technology.
Interest	Interest is a fee paid by a borrower of assets to the owner as a form of compensation for the use of the assets. It is most commonly the price paid for the use of borrowed money, or money earned by deposited funds. When money is borrowed, interest is typically paid to the lender as a percentage of the principal, the amount owed to the lender.

14. GDP: A Measure of Total Production and Income,

CHAPTER HIGHLIGHTS & NOTES: KEY TERMS, PEOPLE, PLACES, CONCEPTS

Market price	In economics, market price is the economic price for which a good or service is offered in the marketplace. It is of interest mainly in the study of microeconomics. Market value and market price are equal only under conditions of market efficiency, equilibrium, and rational expectations.
Index	In economics and finance, an index is a statistical measure of changes in a representative group of individual data points. These data may be derived from any number of sources, including company performance, prices, productivity, and employment. Economic indices (index, plural) track economic health from different perspectives.
Profit	In neoclassical microeconomic theory, the term profit has two related but distinct meanings. Economic profit is similar to accounting profit but smaller because it reflects the total opportunity costs (both explicit and implicit) of a venture to an investor. Normal profit refers to a situation in which the economic profit is zero.
Depreciation	In accountancy, depreciation refers to two aspects of the same concept:•the decrease in value of assets (fair value depreciation), and•the allocation of the cost of assets to periods in which the assets are used (depreciation with the matching principle). The former affects the balance sheet of a business or entity, and the latter affects the net income that they report. Generally the cost is allocated, as depreciation expense, among the periods in which the asset is expected to be used. This expense is recognized by businesses for financial reporting and tax purposes.
Disposable personal income	Disposable income is total personal income minus personal current taxes. In national accounts definitions, personal income minus personal current taxes equals disposable personal income. Subtracting personal outlays (which includes the major category of personal [or private] consumption expenditure) yields personal (or, private) savings, hence the income left after paying away all the taxes is referred to as disposable income.
Gross national product	Gross national product is the market value of all the products and services produced in one year by labor and property supplied by the citizens of a country. Unlike Gross Domestic Product (GDP), which defines production based on the geographical location of production, Gross national product allocates production based on ownership. Gross national product does not distinguish between qualitative improvements in the state of the technical arts (e.g., increasing computer processing speeds), and quantitative increases in goods (e.g., number of computers produced), and considers both to be forms of 'economic growth'.
Production	Production is a process of combining various material inputs and immaterial inputs in order to make something for consumption (the output). It is the act of creating output, a good or service which has value and contributes to the utility of individuals.

14. GDP: A Measure of Total Production and Income,

CHAPTER HIGHLIGHTS & NOTES: KEY TERMS, PEOPLE, PLACES, CONCEPTS

Nominal GDP	Gross domestic product is a monetary measure of the value of all final goods and services produced in a period (quarterly or yearly). Nominal GDP estimates are commonly used to determine the economic performance of a whole country or region, and to make international comparisons. Nominal GDP, however, does not reflect differences in the cost of living and the inflation rates of the countries; therefore using a GDP PPP per capita basis is arguably more useful when comparing differences in living standards between nations.
Real GDP	Real Gross Domestic Product (real GDP) is a macroeconomic measure of the value of economic output adjusted for price changes . This adjustment transforms the money-value measure, nominal GDP, into an index for quantity of total output. GDP is the sum of consumer Spending, Investment made by industry, Excess of Exports over Imports and Government Spending.
Standard of living	Standard of living refers to the level of wealth, comfort, material goods and necessities available to a certain socioeconomic class in a certain geographic area. The standard of living includes factors such as income, quality and availability of employment, class disparity, poverty rate, quality and affordability of housing, hours of work required to purchase necessities, gross domestic product, inflation rate, number of holiday days per year, affordable (or free) access to quality healthcare, quality and availability of education, life expectancy, incidence of disease, cost of goods and services, infrastructure, national economic growth, economic and political and stability, political and religious freedom, environmental quality, climate and safety. The standard of living is closely related to quality of life.
Value	Economic value is a measure of the benefit that an economic actor can gain from either a good or service. It is generally measured relative to units of currency, and the interpretation is therefore 'what is the maximum amount of money a specific actor is willing and able to pay for the good or service'? Note that economic value is not the same as market price. If a consumer is willing to buy a good, it implies that the customer places a higher value on the good than the market price.
Business cycle	The term business cycle refers to economy-wide fluctuations in production, trade and economic activity in general over several months or years in an economy organized on free-enterprise principles. The business cycle is the upward and downward movements of levels of GDP (gross domestic product) and refers to the period of expansions and contractions in the level of economic activities (business fluctuations) around its long-term growth trend. These fluctuations occur around a long-term growth trend, and typically involve shifts over time between periods of relatively rapid economic growth (an expansion or boom), and periods of relative stagnation or decline (a contraction or recession).

14. GDP: A Measure of Total Production and Income,

CHAPTER HIGHLIGHTS & NOTES: KEY TERMS, PEOPLE, PLACES, CONCEPTS

Recession	In economics, a recession is a business cycle contraction. It is a general slowdown in economic activity. Macroeconomic indicators such as GDP (gross domestic product), investment spending, capacity utilization, household income, business profits, and inflation fall, while bankruptcies and the unemployment rate rise.
PHASE	PHASE is a partnership between several international non-governmental organisations registered in Austria, Nepal and the United Kingdom (UK). The organisations specialise in improving health and education services and livelihood opportunities for disadvantaged populations and most of this work takes place in Nepal. PHASE aims to support the most vulnerable (women, children, low castes, the very poor and people with disabilities) to break the cycle of poverty.
Gift	A gift, in the law of property, is the voluntary transfer of property from one person to another (the donee or grantee) without full valuable consideration. In order for a gift to be legally effective, the donor must have intended to give the gift to the donee (donative intent), and the gift must actually be delivered to and accepted by the donee. Gifts can be either:•lifetime gifts (inter vivos gift, donatio inter vivos) - a gift of a present or future interest made and delivered in the donor's lifetime; or•deathbed gifts (gift causa mortis, donatio mortis causa) - a future gift made in expectation of the donor's imminent death.
Hong	The Hongs were major business houses in Canton, China and later Hong Kong with significant influence on patterns of consumerism, trade, manufacturing and other key areas of the economy. They were originally led by Howqua as head of the cohong.
International Monetary Fund	The International Monetary Fund is an international organization that was initiated in 1944 at the Bretton Woods Conference and formally created in 1945 by 29 member countries. The International Monetary Fund's stated goal was to assist in the reconstruction of the world's international payment system post-World War II. Countries contribute funds to a pool through a quota system from which countries with payment imbalances temporarily can borrow monies and other resources. As of the 14th General Review of Quotas in late 2010 the fund stood at SDR476.8bn, or about US$755.7bn at then-current exchange rates.
Purchasing power	Purchasing power is the number of goods or services that can be purchased with a unit of currency. For example, if one had taken one unit of currency to a store in the 1950s, it is probable that it would have been possible to buy a greater number of items than would today, indicating that one would have had a greater purchasing power in the 1950s. Currency can be either a commodity money, like gold or silver, or fiat currency, or free-floating market-valued currency like US dollars.
Purchasing power parity	Purchasing power parity is a component of some economic theories and is a technique used to determine the relative value of different currencies.

14. GDP: A Measure of Total Production and Income,

CHAPTER HIGHLIGHTS & NOTES: KEY TERMS, PEOPLE, PLACES, CONCEPTS

	Theories that invoke purchasing power parity assume that in some circumstances (for example, as a long-run tendency) it would cost exactly the same number of, say, US dollars to buy euros and then to use the proceeds to buy a market basket of goods as it would cost to use those dollars directly in purchasing the market basket of goods.
	The concept of purchasing power parity allows one to estimate what the exchange rate between two currencies would have to be in order for the exchange to be at par with the purchasing power of the two countries' currencies.
Nature	Nature is a concept with two major sets of inter-related meanings, referring on the one hand to the things which are natural, or subject to the normal working of 'laws of nature', or on the other hand to the essential properties and causes of those things to be what they naturally are, or in other words the laws of nature themselves.
	How to understand the meaning and significance of nature has been a consistent theme of discussion within the history of Western Civilization, in the philosophical fields of metaphysics and epistemology, as well as in theology and science. The study of natural things and the regular laws which seem to govern them, as opposed to discussion about what it means to be natural, is the area of natural science.
EDGAR	EDGAR, the Electronic Data-Gathering, Analysis, and Retrieval system, performs automated collection, validation, indexing, acceptance, and forwarding of submissions by companies and others who are required by law to file forms with the U.S. Securities and Exchange Commission (the 'SEC'). The database is freely available to the public via the Internet (Web or FTP).
Household	A household consists of one or more people who live in the same dwelling and also share at meals or living accommodation, and may consist of a single family or some other grouping of people. A single dwelling will be considered to contain multiple households if meals or living space are not shared. The household is the basic unit of analysis in many social, microeconomic and government models, and is important to the fields of economics, inheritance.
Underground	The underground was a countercultural movement in the United Kingdom linked to the underground culture in the United States and associated with the hippie phenomenon. Its primary focus was around Ladbroke Grove and Notting Hill in London. It generated its own magazines and newspapers, bands, clubs and alternative lifestyle, associated with cannabis and LSD use and a strong socio-political revolutionary agenda to create an alternative society.
Life expectancy	Life expectancy is the expected number of years of life remaining at a given age. It is denoted by e_x, which means the average number of subsequent years of life for someone now aged x, according to a particular mortality experience.

14. GDP: A Measure of Total Production and Income,

CHAPTER HIGHLIGHTS & NOTES: KEY TERMS, PEOPLE, PLACES, CONCEPTS

Social justice	Social justice is the ability people have to realize their potential in the society where they live. Classically, 'justice' (especially corrective justice or distributive justice) referred to ensuring that individuals both fulfilled their societal roles, and received what was due from society. 'Social justice' is generally used to refer to a set of institutions which will enable people to lead a fulfilling life and be active contributors to their community.
Price level	The general price level is a hypothetical measure of overall prices for some set of goods and services, in a given region during a given interval, normalized relative to some base set. Typically, a price level is approximated with a price index.
Relative price	A relative price is the price of a commodity such as a good or service in terms of another; i.e., the ratio of two prices. A relative price may be expressed in terms of a ratio between any two prices or the ratio between the price of one particular good and a weighted average of all other goods available in the market. A relative price is an opportunity cost.
Relative	•Kinship, the principle binding the most basic social units society. If two people are connected by circumstances of birth, they are said to be relatives Philosophy•Relativism, the concept that points of view have no absolute truth or validity, having only relative, subjective value according to differences in perception and consideration, or relatively, as in the relative value of an object to a person •Relative value (philosophy) Economics/Hindustan•Relative value (economics) Popular culture Film and television•Relatively Speaking (1965 play), 1965 British play •Relatively Speaking (game show), late 1980s television game show •Everything's Relative#Yu-Gi-Oh! (Yu-Gi-Oh! Duel Monsters), 2000 Japanese anime Yu-Gi-Oh! Duel Monsters episode •Relative Values, 2000 film based on the play of the same name. •It's All Relative, 2003-4 comedy television series •Intelligence is Relative, tag line for the 2008 film Burn After Reading Music•Friends & Relatives, 1999 compilation album •Dead Relatives, 2000 music album by Canadian Emm Gryner •Relative Ways, 2001 music album by ...And You Will Know Us by the Trail of Dead Physics Relative is a term used in physics, and especially in Special and General relativity, to denote that something is dependent on a reference frame, or that it is taken specifically in a given reference frame - 'Its velocity relative to the cow is 15.5m/s', 'Time and Space are relative, not fixed.'

14. GDP: A Measure of Total Production and Income,

CHAPTER QUIZ: KEY TERMS, PEOPLE, PLACES, CONCEPTS

1. In economics, the terms _____ of income or _____ refer to a simple economic model which describes the reciprocal circulation of income between producers and consumers. In the _____ model, the inter-dependent entities of producer and consumer are referred to as 'firms' and 'households' respectively and provide each other with factors in order to facilitate the flow of income. Firms provide consumers with goods and services in exchange for consumer expenditure and 'factors of production' from households.

    a. cohesion funds European Union
    b. Benefit incidence
    c. Blanket order
    d. Circular flow

2. An _____ or economic system consists of the production, distribution or trade, and consumption of limited goods and services by different agents in a given geographical location. The economic agents can be individuals, businesses, organizations, or governments. Transactions occur when two parties agree to the value or price of the transacted good or service, commonly expressed in a certain currency.

    a. Care work
    b. Cash collection
    c. Economy
    d. Commodity production

3. A _____ was a type of silver coinage of France from the time of Saint Louis. There were _____ tournois and _____ parisis. The _____ was sub-divided in half _____ and quarter _____.

    a. 1 kroon coin
    b. Gros
    c. Bon
    d. British Numismatic Society

4. In common usage, an expense or _____ is an outflow of money to another person or group to pay for an item or service, or for a category of costs. For a tenant, rent is an expense. For students or parents, tuition is an expense.

    a. Expenditure
    b. Cigar Box Method
    c. Cash crop
    d. Casa grande

5. . In economics, any commodity which is produced and subsequently consumed by the consumer, to satisfy its current wants or needs, is a consumer good or _____. Consumer goods are goods that are ultimately consumed rather than used in the production of another good. For example, a microwave oven or a bicycle which is sold to a consumer is a _____ or consumer good, whereas the components which are sold to be used in those goods are called intermediate goods.

    a. Bad
    b. Cargo

14. GDP: A Measure of Total Production and Income,
CHAPTER QUIZ: KEY TERMS, PEOPLE, PLACES, CONCEPTS

c. Final good
d. Club good

ANSWER KEY
14. GDP: A Measure of Total Production and Income,

1. d
2. c
3. b
4. a
5. c

You can take the complete Online Interactive Chapter Practice Test

for 14. GDP: A Measure of Total Production and Income,
on all key terms, persons, places, and concepts.

No Additional Costs

http://www.Cram101.com

Register, send an email request to Travis.Reese@Cram101.com to get your user Id and password.

Include your customer order number, and ISBN number from your studyguide Retailer.

15. Jobs and Unemployment,

CHAPTER OUTLINE: KEY TERMS, PEOPLE, PLACES, CONCEPTS

	Labor force
	Rate
	Discouraged worker
	Labor force participation rate
	Great Depression
	Labor market
	Eurozone
	Gift
	Hong
	Recession
	Economic growth
	Nature
	Unemployment
	Market economy
	Part-time
	Frictional unemployment
	Structural unemployment
	Full employment
	Real wage
	Structural change
	Real GDP

15. Jobs and Unemployment,
CHAPTER OUTLINE: KEY TERMS, PEOPLE, PLACES, CONCEPTS

	Output gap
	Employment
	Status

CHAPTER HIGHLIGHTS & NOTES: KEY TERMS, PEOPLE, PLACES, CONCEPTS

Labor force	The labor force is the actual number of people available for work. The labor force of a country includes both the employed and the unemployed. The labor force participation rate, LFPR (or economic activity rate, EAR), is the ratio between the labor force and the overall size of their cohort (national population of the same age range).
Rate	In mathematics, a rate is a ratio between two measurements with different units. If the unit or quantity in respect of which something is changing is not specified, usually the rate is per unit time. However, a rate of change can be specified per unit time, or per unit of length or mass or another quantity.
Discouraged worker	Not to be confused with Disgruntled worker. In economics, a discouraged worker is a person of legal employment age who is not actively seeking employment or who does not find employment after long-term unemployment. This is usually because an individual has given up looking or has had no success in finding a job, hence the term 'discouraged'.
Labor force participation rate	The labor force is the actual number of people available for work. The labor force of a country includes both the employed and the unemployed. The labor force participation rate, labor force participation rate (or economic activity rate, EAR), is the ratio between the labor force and the overall size of their cohort (national population of the same age range).
Great Depression	The Great Depression was a severe worldwide economic depression in the decade preceding World War II. The timing of the Great Depression varied across nations, but in most countries it started in 1930 and lasted until the late 1930s or middle 1940s. It was the longest, deepest, and most widespread depression of the 20th century.

15. Jobs and Unemployment,

CHAPTER HIGHLIGHTS & NOTES: KEY TERMS, PEOPLE, PLACES, CONCEPTS

Labor market	Labor economics seeks to understand the functioning and dynamics of the markets for wage labor. Labor markets or job markets function through the interaction of workers and employers. Labor economics looks at the suppliers of labor services (workers), the demands of labor services (employers), and attempts to understand the resulting pattern of wages, employment, and income.
Eurozone	The eurozone, officially called the euro area, is an economic and monetary union (EMU) of 18 European Union (EU) member states that have adopted the euro (€) as their common currency and sole legal tender. The eurozone currently consists of Austria, Belgium, Cyprus, Estonia, Finland, France, Germany, Greece, Ireland, Italy, Latvia, Luxembourg, Malta, the Netherlands, Portugal, Slovakia, Slovenia, and Spain. Other EU states (except for the United Kingdom and Denmark) are obliged to join once they meet the criteria to do so.
Gift	A gift, in the law of property, is the voluntary transfer of property from one person to another (the donee or grantee) without full valuable consideration. In order for a gift to be legally effective, the donor must have intended to give the gift to the donee (donative intent), and the gift must actually be delivered to and accepted by the donee. Gifts can be either:•lifetime gifts (inter vivos gift, donatio inter vivos) - a gift of a present or future interest made and delivered in the donor's lifetime; or•deathbed gifts (gift causa mortis, donatio mortis causa) - a future gift made in expectation of the donor's imminent death.
Hong	The Hongs were major business houses in Canton, China and later Hong Kong with significant influence on patterns of consumerism, trade, manufacturing and other key areas of the economy. They were originally led by Howqua as head of the cohong.
Recession	In economics, a recession is a business cycle contraction. It is a general slowdown in economic activity. Macroeconomic indicators such as GDP (gross domestic product), investment spending, capacity utilization, household income, business profits, and inflation fall, while bankruptcies and the unemployment rate rise.
Economic growth	Economic growth is the increase in the market value of the goods and services produced by an economy over time. It is conventionally measured as the percent rate of increase in real gross domestic product, or real GDP. Of more importance is the growth of the ratio of GDP to population (GDP per capita), which is also called per capita income. An increase in per capita income is referred to as intensive growth.
Nature	Nature is a concept with two major sets of inter-related meanings, referring on the one hand to the things which are natural, or subject to the normal working of 'laws of nature', or on the other hand to the essential properties and causes of those things to be what they naturally are, or in other words the laws of nature themselves.

15. Jobs and Unemployment,

CHAPTER HIGHLIGHTS & NOTES: KEY TERMS, PEOPLE, PLACES, CONCEPTS

	How to understand the meaning and significance of nature has been a consistent theme of discussion within the history of Western Civilization, in the philosophical fields of metaphysics and epistemology, as well as in theology and science. The study of natural things and the regular laws which seem to govern them, as opposed to discussion about what it means to be natural, is the area of natural science.
Unemployment	Unemployment occurs when people are without work and actively seeking work. The unemployment rate is a measure of the prevalence of unemployment and it is calculated as a percentage by dividing the number of unemployed individuals by all individuals currently in the labor force. During periods of recession, an economy usually experiences a relatively high unemployment rate.
Market economy	Manorialism, an essential element of feudal society, was the organizing principle of rural economy that originated in the villa system of the Late Roman Empire, was widely practiced in medieval western and parts of central Europe, and was slowly replaced by the advent of a money-based market economy and new forms of agrarian contract.
	Manorialism was characterised by the vesting of legal and economic power in a Lord of the Manor, supported economically from his own direct landholding in a manor, and from the obligatory contributions of a legally subject part of the peasant population under the jurisdiction of himself and his manorial court. These obligations could be payable in several ways, in labor (the French term corvée is conventionally applied), in kind, or, on rare occasions, in coin.
Part-time	A part-time contract is a form of employment that carries fewer hours per week than a full-time job. They work in shifts but remain on call while off duty and during annual leave. The shifts are often rotational.
Frictional unemployment	Frictional unemployment is the time period between jobs when a worker is searching for, or transitioning from one job to another. It is sometimes called search unemployment and can be voluntary based on the circumstances of the unemployed individual.
Structural unemployment	Structural unemployment is a form of unemployment where, at a given wage, the quantity of labor supplied exceeds the quantity of labor demanded, because there is a fundamental mismatch between the number of people who want to work and the number of jobs that are available. The unemployed workers may lack the skills needed for the jobs, or they may not live in the part of the country or world where the jobs are available. Structural unemployment is one of the five major categories of unemployment distinguished by economists.
Full employment	Full employment, in macroeconomics, is the level of employment rates where there is no cyclical or deficient-demand unemployment. It is defined by the majority of mainstream economists as being an acceptable level of unemployment somewhere above 0%.

15. Jobs and Unemployment,

CHAPTER HIGHLIGHTS & NOTES: KEY TERMS, PEOPLE, PLACES, CONCEPTS

Real wage	The term real wages refers to wages that have been adjusted for inflation, or, equivalently, wages in terms of the amount of goods and services that can be bought. This term is used in contrast to nominal wages or unadjusted wages. Because it has been adjusted to account for changes in the prices of goods and services, real wages provide a clearer representation of an individual's wages in terms of what they can afford to buy with those wages - specifically, in terms of the amount of goods and services that can be bought.
Structural change	Economic structural change refers to a long-term shift in the fundamental structure of an economy, which is often linked to growth and economic development. For example, a subsistence economy may be transformed into a manufacturing economy, or a regulated mixed economy is liberalized. A current driver of structural change in the world economy is globalization.
Real GDP	Real Gross Domestic Product (real GDP) is a macroeconomic measure of the value of economic output adjusted for price changes . This adjustment transforms the money-value measure, nominal GDP, into an index for quantity of total output. GDP is the sum of consumer Spending, Investment made by industry, Excess of Exports over Imports and Government Spending.
Output gap	The GDP gap or the output gap is the difference between actual GDP or actual output and potential GDP. The calculation for the output gap is Y-Y* where Y is actual output and Y* is potential output. If this calculation yields a positive number it is called an inflationary gap and indicates the growth of aggregate demand is outpacing the growth of aggregate supply--possibly creating inflation; if the calculation yields a negative number it is called a recessionary gap--possibly signifying deflation. The percentage GDP gap is the actual GDP minus the potential GDP divided by the potential GDP. $$\frac{(GDP_{actual} - GDP_{potential})}{GDP_{potential}}$$
Employment	Employment is a relationship between two parties, usually based on a contract, one being the employer and the other being the employee.
Status	An Individual's status is a legal position held in regards to the rest of the community and not by an act of law or by the consensual acts of the parties, and it is in rem, i.e. these conditions must be recognised by the world. It is the qualities of universality and permanence that distinguish status from consensual relationships such as employment and agency. Hence, a person's status and its attributes are set by the law of the domicile if born in a common law state, or by the law of nationality if born in a civil law state and this status and its attendant capacities should be recognised wherever the person may later travel.

15. Jobs and Unemployment,

CHAPTER QUIZ: KEY TERMS, PEOPLE, PLACES, CONCEPTS

1. The _____, officially called the euro area, is an economic and monetary union (EMU) of 18 European Union (EU) member states that have adopted the euro (€) as their common currency and sole legal tender. The _____ currently consists of Austria, Belgium, Cyprus, Estonia, Finland, France, Germany, Greece, Ireland, Italy, Latvia, Luxembourg, Malta, the Netherlands, Portugal, Slovakia, Slovenia, and Spain. Other EU states (except for the United Kingdom and Denmark) are obliged to join once they meet the criteria to do so.

    a. Fuel protests in the United Kingdom
    b. Battle of Annaberg
    c. Eurozone
    d. Freikorps Oberland

2. In mathematics, a _____ is a ratio between two measurements with different units. If the unit or quantity in respect of which something is changing is not specified, usually the _____ is per unit time. However, a _____ of change can be specified per unit time, or per unit of length or mass or another quantity.

    a. Bank rate
    b. Rate
    c. Cash accumulation equation
    d. Coupon leverage

3. The _____ is the actual number of people available for work. The _____ of a country includes both the employed and the unemployed. The _____ participation rate, LFPR (or economic activity rate, EAR), is the ratio between the _____ and the overall size of their cohort (national population of the same age range).

    a. Dual labour market
    b. Labor force
    c. Gender pay gap in Australia
    d. Get Britain Working

4. Not to be confused with Disgruntled worker.

    In economics, a _____ is a person of legal employment age who is not actively seeking employment or who does not find employment after long-term unemployment. This is usually because an individual has given up looking or has had no success in finding a job, hence the term 'discouraged'.

    a. Discouraged worker
    b. Benefit incidence
    c. Blanket order
    d. Bond

5. . The labor force is the actual number of people available for work. The labor force of a country includes both the employed and the unemployed. The _____, _____ (or economic activity rate, EAR), is the ratio between the labor force and the overall size of their cohort (national population of the same age range).

15. Jobs and Unemployment,

CHAPTER QUIZ: KEY TERMS, PEOPLE, PLACES, CONCEPTS

a. Dual labour market
b. Full Employment in a Free Society
c. Labor force participation rate
d. Get Britain Working

ANSWER KEY
15. Jobs and Unemployment,

1. c
2. b
3. b
4. a
5. c

You can take the complete Online Interactive Chapter Practice Test

for 15. Jobs and Unemployment,
on all key terms, persons, places, and concepts.

No Additional Costs

http://www.Cram101.com

Register, send an email request to Travis.Reese@Cram101.com to get your user Id and password.

Include your customer order number, and ISBN number from your studyguide Retailer.

16. The CPI and the Cost of Living,

CHAPTER OUTLINE: KEY TERMS, PEOPLE, PLACES, CONCEPTS

- Consumer
- Consumer price index
- Price index
- Basket
- Consumption
- Good
- Goods and services
- Market basket
- Service
- Deflation
- Rate
- Depression
- Great Depression
- Hong
- Inferior good
- Economic growth
- Inflation
- Cost
- Price
- Price level
- Bias

16. The CPI and the Cost of Living,
CHAPTER OUTLINE: KEY TERMS, PEOPLE, PLACES, CONCEPTS

| Import
| Sources
| Purchasing power
| Quality
| Core inflation
| Gros
| Core
| Index
| Nominal GDP
| Real GDP
| Value
| Wedge
| Real wage
| Nominal interest rate
| Real interest rate
| Interest rate

16. The CPI and the Cost of Living,

CHAPTER HIGHLIGHTS & NOTES: KEY TERMS, PEOPLE, PLACES, CONCEPTS

Consumer	A consumer is a person or group of people, such as a household, who are the final users of products or services. The consumer's use is final in the sense that the product is usually not improved by the use.
Consumer price index	A consumer price index measures changes in the price level of a market basket of consumer goods and services purchased by households. The Consumer price index in the United States is defined by the Bureau of Labor Statistics as 'a measure of the average change over time in the prices paid by urban consumers for a market basket of consumer goods and services.' The Consumer price index is a statistical estimate constructed using the prices of a sample of representative items whose prices are collected periodically. Sub-indexes and sub-sub-indexes are computed for different categories and sub-categories of goods and services, being combined to produce the overall index with weights reflecting their shares in the total of the consumer expenditures covered by the index.
Price index	A price index is a normalized average of price relatives for a given class of goods or services in a given region, during a given interval of time. It is a statistic designed to help to compare how these price relatives, taken as a whole, differ between time periods or geographical locations. Price indexes have several potential uses.
Basket	A basket is an economic term for a group of several securities created for the purpose of simultaneous buying or selling. Baskets are frequently used for program trading. Certain specific products can be seen as specialized 'baskets'.
Consumption	Consumption is a major concept in economics and is also studied by many other social sciences. Economists are particularly interested in the relationship between consumption and income, and therefore in economics the consumption function plays a major role. Different schools of economists define production and consumption differently.
Good	In economics, a good is a material that satisfies human wants and provides utility, for example, to a consumer making a purchase. A common distinction is made between 'goods' that are tangible property (also called goods) and services, which are non-physical. Commodities may be used as a synonym for economic goods but often refer to marketable raw materials and primary products.
Goods and services	In economics, goods and services are the outcome of human efforts to meet the wants and needs of people. Economic output is divided into physical goods and intangible services. Goods are items that can be seen and touched, such as books, pens, salt, shoes, hats, and folders.

16. The CPI and the Cost of Living,

CHAPTER HIGHLIGHTS & NOTES: KEY TERMS, PEOPLE, PLACES, CONCEPTS

Market basket	The term market basket or commodity bundle refers to a fixed list of items used specifically to track the progress of inflation in an economy or specific market.
Service	In economics, a service is an intangible commodity. That is, services are an example of intangible economic goods. Service provision is often an economic activity where the buyer does not generally, except by exclusive contract, obtain exclusive ownership of the thing purchased.
Deflation	In economics, deflation is a decrease in the general price level of goods and services. Deflation occurs when the inflation rate falls below 0% (a negative inflation rate). This should not be confused with disinflation, a slow-down in the inflation rate (i.e., when inflation declines to lower levels).
Rate	In mathematics, a rate is a ratio between two measurements with different units. If the unit or quantity in respect of which something is changing is not specified, usually the rate is per unit time. However, a rate of change can be specified per unit time, or per unit of length or mass or another quantity.
Depression	In economics, a depression is a sustained, long-term downturn in economic activity in one or more economies. It is a more severe downturn than a recession, which is seen by some economists as inevitable part of capitalist economy. Considered by some economists to be a rare and extreme form of recession, a depression is characterized by its length; by abnormally large increases in unemployment; falls in the availability of credit, often due to some kind of banking or financial crisis; shrinking output as buyers dry up and suppliers cut back on production and investment; large number of bankruptcies including sovereign debt defaults; significantly reduced amounts of trade and commerce, especially international; as well as highly volatile relative currency value fluctuations, most often due to devaluations.
Great Depression	The Great Depression was a severe worldwide economic depression in the decade preceding World War II. The timing of the Great Depression varied across nations, but in most countries it started in 1930 and lasted until the late 1930s or middle 1940s. It was the longest, deepest, and most widespread depression of the 20th century. In the 21st century, the Great Depression is commonly used as an example of how far the world's economy can decline.
Hong	The Hongs were major business houses in Canton, China and later Hong Kong with significant influence on patterns of consumerism, trade, manufacturing and other key areas of the economy. They were originally led by Howqua as head of the cohong.

16. The CPI and the Cost of Living,

CHAPTER HIGHLIGHTS & NOTES: KEY TERMS, PEOPLE, PLACES, CONCEPTS

Inferior good	In economics, an inferior good is a good that decreases in demand when consumer income rises, unlike normal goods, for which the opposite is observed. Normal goods are those for which consumers' demand increases when their income increases. This would be the opposite of a superior good, one that is often associated with wealth and the wealthy, whereas an inferior good is often associated with lower socio-economic groups.
Economic growth	Economic growth is the increase in the market value of the goods and services produced by an economy over time. It is conventionally measured as the percent rate of increase in real gross domestic product, or real GDP. Of more importance is the growth of the ratio of GDP to population (GDP per capita), which is also called per capita income. An increase in per capita income is referred to as intensive growth.
Inflation	In economics, inflation is a sustained increase in the general price level of goods and services in an economy over a period of time. When the general price level rises, each unit of currency buys fewer goods and services. Consequently, inflation reflects a reduction in the purchasing power per unit of money - a loss of real value in the medium of exchange and unit of account within the economy.
Cost	In production, research, retail, and accounting, a cost is the value of money that has been used up to produce something, and hence is not available for use anymore. In business, the cost may be one of acquisition, in which case the amount of money expended to acquire it is counted as cost. In this case, money is the input that is gone in order to acquire the thing.
Price	In ordinary usage, price is the quantity of payment or compensation given by one party to another in return for goods or services. In modern economies, prices are generally expressed in units of some form of currency. (For commodities, they are expressed as currency per unit weight of the commodity, e.g. euros per kilogram).
Price level	The general price level is a hypothetical measure of overall prices for some set of goods and services, in a given region during a given interval, normalized relative to some base set. Typically, a price level is approximated with a price index.
Bias	A statistic is biased if it is calculated in such a way that it is systematically different from the population parameter of interest. The following lists some types of biases, which can overlap. •Selection bias,involves individuals being more likely to be selected for study than others, biasing the sample.
Import	An import is a good brought into a jurisdiction, especially across a national border, from an external source. The purchaser of the exotic good is called an importer. An import in the receiving country is an export from the sending country.

16. The CPI and the Cost of Living,

CHAPTER HIGHLIGHTS & NOTES: KEY TERMS, PEOPLE, PLACES, CONCEPTS

Sources	Sources is a web portal for journalists, freelance writers, editors, authors and researchers, focusing especially on human sources: experts and spokespersons who are prepared to answer reporters' questions or make themselves available for on-air interviews.
Purchasing power	Purchasing power is the number of goods or services that can be purchased with a unit of currency. For example, if one had taken one unit of currency to a store in the 1950s, it is probable that it would have been possible to buy a greater number of items than would today, indicating that one would have had a greater purchasing power in the 1950s. Currency can be either a commodity money, like gold or silver, or fiat currency, or free-floating market-valued currency like US dollars.
Quality	Quality in business, engineering and manufacturing has a pragmatic interpretation as the non-inferiority or superiority of something; it is also defined as fitness for purpose. Quality is a perceptual, conditional, and somewhat subjective attribute and may be understood differently by different people. Consumers may focus on the specification quality of a product/service, or how it compares to competitors in the marketplace.
Core inflation	Core inflation represents the long run trend in the price level. In measuring long run inflation, transitory price changes should be excluded. One way of accomplishing this is by excluding items frequently subject to volatile prices, like food and energy.
Gros	A gros was a type of silver coinage of France from the time of Saint Louis. There were gros tournois and gros parisis. The gros was sub-divided in half gros and quarter gros.
Core	In game theory, the core is the set of feasible allocations that cannot be improved upon by a subset of the economy's consumers. A coalition is said to improve upon or block a feasible allocation if the members of that coalition are better off under another feasible allocation that is identical to the first except that every member of the coalition has a different consumption bundle that is part of an aggregate consumption bundle that can be constructed from publicly available technology and the initial endowments of each consumer in the coalition. An allocation is said to have the core property if there is no coalition that can improve upon it.
Index	In economics and finance, an index is a statistical measure of changes in a representative group of individual data points. These data may be derived from any number of sources, including company performance, prices, productivity, and employment. Economic indices (index, plural) track economic health from different perspectives.
Nominal GDP	Gross domestic product is a monetary measure of the value of all final goods and services produced in a period (quarterly or yearly). Nominal GDP estimates are commonly used to determine the economic performance of a whole country or region, and to make international comparisons.

16. The CPI and the Cost of Living,

CHAPTER HIGHLIGHTS & NOTES: KEY TERMS, PEOPLE, PLACES, CONCEPTS

Real GDP	Real Gross Domestic Product (real GDP) is a macroeconomic measure of the value of economic output adjusted for price changes. This adjustment transforms the money-value measure, nominal GDP, into an index for quantity of total output. GDP is the sum of consumer Spending, Investment made by industry, Excess of Exports over Imports and Government Spending.
Value	Economic value is a measure of the benefit that an economic actor can gain from either a good or service. It is generally measured relative to units of currency, and the interpretation is therefore 'what is the maximum amount of money a specific actor is willing and able to pay for the good or service'?
	Note that economic value is not the same as market price. If a consumer is willing to buy a good, it implies that the customer places a higher value on the good than the market price.
Wedge	In solid geometry, a wedge is a polyhedron defined by two triangles and three trapezoid faces. A wedge has five faces, nine edges, and six vertices.
	A wedge is a subclass of the prismatoids with the base and opposite ridge in two parallel planes.
Real wage	The term real wages refers to wages that have been adjusted for inflation, or, equivalently, wages in terms of the amount of goods and services that can be bought. This term is used in contrast to nominal wages or unadjusted wages. Because it has been adjusted to account for changes in the prices of goods and services, real wages provide a clearer representation of an individual's wages in terms of what they can afford to buy with those wages - specifically, in terms of the amount of goods and services that can be bought.
Nominal interest rate	In finance and economics, nominal interest rate or nominal rate of interest refers to two distinct things: the rate of interest before adjustment for inflation ; or, for interest rates 'as stated' without adjustment for the full effect of compounding (also referred to as the nominal annual rate). An interest rate is called nominal if the frequency of compounding (e.g. a month) is not identical to the basic time unit (normally a year).
Real interest rate	The real interest rate is the rate of interest an investor expects to receive after allowing for inflation. It can be described more formally by the Fisher equation, which states that the real interest rate is approximately the nominal interest rate minus the inflation rate. If, for example, an investor were able to lock in a 5% interest rate for the coming year and anticipated a 2% rise in prices, they would expect to earn a real interest rate of 3%.
Interest rate	An interest rate is the rate at which interest is paid by a borrower for the use of money that they borrow from a lender (creditor). Specifically, the interest rate is a percent of principal (P) paid a certain amount of times (m) per period (usually quoted per annum).

16. The CPI and the Cost of Living,

CHAPTER QUIZ: KEY TERMS, PEOPLE, PLACES, CONCEPTS

1. The _____ was a severe worldwide economic depression in the decade preceding World War II. The timing of the _____ varied across nations, but in most countries it started in 1930 and lasted until the late 1930s or middle 1940s. It was the longest, deepest, and most widespread depression of the 20th century.

    In the 21st century, the _____ is commonly used as an example of how far the world's economy can decline.

    a. Great Depression
    b. Bank failure
    c. Jewish Social Democratic Party
    d. Communist Bund

2. In solid geometry, a _____ is a polyhedron defined by two triangles and three trapezoid faces. A _____ has five faces, nine edges, and six vertices.

    A _____ is a subclass of the prismatoids with the base and opposite ridge in two parallel planes.

    a. Bicupola
    b. Wedge
    c. Bipyramid
    d. Bitruncation

3. In economics, _____ is a decrease in the general price level of goods and services. _____ occurs when the inflation rate falls below 0% (a negative inflation rate). This should not be confused with disinflation, a slow-down in the inflation rate (i.e., when inflation declines to lower levels).

    a. Deflation
    b. Modern Monetary Theory
    c. Monetary inflation
    d. Target Two Point Zero

4. A _____ is a person or group of people, such as a household, who are the final users of products or services. The _____'s use is final in the sense that the product is usually not improved by the use.

    a. Bliss point
    b. Budget constraint
    c. Budget set
    d. Consumer

5. . An _____ is a good brought into a jurisdiction, especially across a national border, from an external source. The purchaser of the exotic good is called an importer. An _____ in the receiving country is an export from the sending country.

    a. Balanced trade
    b. Import

16. The CPI and the Cost of Living,

CHAPTER QUIZ: KEY TERMS, PEOPLE, PLACES, CONCEPTS

c. Banana Framework Agreement
d. Bilateral trade

ANSWER KEY
16. The CPI and the Cost of Living,

1. a
2. b
3. a
4. d
5. b

You can take the complete Online Interactive Chapter Practice Test

for 16. The CPI and the Cost of Living,
on all key terms, persons, places, and concepts.

No Additional Costs

http://www.Cram101.com

Register, send an email request to Travis.Reese@Cram101.com to get your user Id and password.

Include your customer order number, and ISBN number from your studyguide Retailer.

17. Potential GDP and Economic Growth,

CHAPTER OUTLINE: KEY TERMS, PEOPLE, PLACES, CONCEPTS

- Capitalism
- Employment
- Interest
- Money
- Socialism
- Theory
- Great Depression
- Recession
- Monetarist
- European Union
- Factor
- Factors of production
- Gift
- Hong
- Economic growth
- Nature
- Diminishing returns
- Production function
- Demand
- Labor force
- Supply

17. Potential GDP and Economic Growth,
CHAPTER OUTLINE: KEY TERMS, PEOPLE, PLACES, CONCEPTS

_____ Labor market

_____ Real wage

_____ Participation

_____ Full employment

_____ Unemployment

_____ Productivity

_____ Rate

_____ Real GDP

_____ Standard of living

_____ Bradford

_____ Industrial Revolution

_____ Executive officer

_____ Investment

_____ Saving

_____ Economic policy

_____ Human capital

_____ Information revolution

_____ Sources

_____ Information Age

_____ Internet

_____ Advance

17. Potential GDP and Economic Growth,

CHAPTER OUTLINE: KEY TERMS, PEOPLE, PLACES, CONCEPTS

	Consumer
	Economic freedom
	Property rights
	Market
	Circular flow
	International trade
	Outsourcing
	Quality
	Trade

CHAPTER HIGHLIGHTS & NOTES: KEY TERMS, PEOPLE, PLACES, CONCEPTS

Capitalism	Capitalism is an economic system in which trade, industry and the means of production are controlled by private owners with the goal of making profits in a market economy. Central characteristics of capitalism include capital accumulation, competitive markets and wage labor. In a capitalist economy, the parties to a transaction typically determine the prices at which assets, goods, and services are exchanged.
Employment	Employment is a relationship between two parties, usually based on a contract, one being the employer and the other being the employee.
Interest	Interest is a fee paid by a borrower of assets to the owner as a form of compensation for the use of the assets. It is most commonly the price paid for the use of borrowed money, or money earned by deposited funds. When money is borrowed, interest is typically paid to the lender as a percentage of the principal, the amount owed to the lender.

17. Potential GDP and Economic Growth,

CHAPTER HIGHLIGHTS & NOTES: KEY TERMS, PEOPLE, PLACES, CONCEPTS

Money	Monetary disequilibrium theory is basically a product of the Monetarist school mainly represented in the works of Leland Yeager and Austrian macroeconomics. The basic concept of monetary equilibrium (disequilibrium) was, however, defined in terms of an individual's demand for cash balance by Mises (1912) in his Theory of Money and Credit. Monetary Disequilibrium is one of three theories of macroeconomic fluctuations which accord an important role to money, the others being the Austrian theory of the business cycle and one based on rational expectations.
Socialism	Socialism is a social and economic system characterised by social ownership of the means of production and co-operative management of the economy, as well as a political theory and movement that aims at the establishment of such a system. 'Social ownership' may refer to cooperative enterprises, common ownership, state ownership, citizen ownership of equity, or any combination of these. There are many varieties of socialism and there is no single definition encapsulating all of them.
Theory	Theory is a group of ideas meant to explain a certain topic of science, such as a single or collection of fact, event(s), or phenomen(a)(on). Typically, a theory is developed through the use of contemplative and rational forms of abstract and generalized thinking. Furthermore, a theory is often based on general principles that are independent of the thing being explained.
Great Depression	The Great Depression was a severe worldwide economic depression in the decade preceding World War II. The timing of the Great Depression varied across nations, but in most countries it started in 1930 and lasted until the late 1930s or middle 1940s. It was the longest, deepest, and most widespread depression of the 20th century. In the 21st century, the Great Depression is commonly used as an example of how far the world's economy can decline.
Recession	In economics, a recession is a business cycle contraction. It is a general slowdown in economic activity. Macroeconomic indicators such as GDP (gross domestic product), investment spending, capacity utilization, household income, business profits, and inflation fall, while bankruptcies and the unemployment rate rise.
Monetarist	A monetarist emphasizes the role of governments in controlling the amount of money in circulation. Monetarist theory asserts that variations in the money supply have major influences on national output in the short run and on price levels over longer periods. Monetarists assert that the objectives of monetary policy are best met by targeting the growth rate of the money supply rather than by engaging in discretionary monetary policy.
European Union	The European Union is a union of 28 member states located primarily in the Europe.

17. Potential GDP and Economic Growth,

CHAPTER HIGHLIGHTS & NOTES: KEY TERMS, PEOPLE, PLACES, CONCEPTS

	With over 500 million inhabitants, it represents 7.3% of the world population, making it the second most populous democracy and first supranational union in the world. The EU is the seventh largest territory by area, extending clockwise direction lies the North, Baltic, Black and Mediterranean Sea and the Atlantic Ocean.
Factor	A factor, Latin for 'doer, maker', is a mercantile fiduciary who receives and sells goods on commission (called factorage), transacting business in his own name and not disclosing his principal, and historically with his seat at a factory (trading post). A factor differs from a commission merchant in that a factor takes possession of goods (or documents of title representing goods) on consignment, whereas a commission merchant sells goods not in his possession on the basis of samples. Most modern factor business is in the textile field, but factors are also used to a great extent in the shoe, furniture, hardware, and other industries, and the trade areas in which factors operate have increased.
Factors of production	In economics, factors of production are the inputs to the production process. Finished goods are the output. Input determines the quantity of output i.e. output depends upon input.
Gift	A gift, in the law of property, is the voluntary transfer of property from one person to another (the donee or grantee) without full valuable consideration. In order for a gift to be legally effective, the donor must have intended to give the gift to the donee (donative intent), and the gift must actually be delivered to and accepted by the donee.
	Gifts can be either:•lifetime gifts (inter vivos gift, donatio inter vivos) - a gift of a present or future interest made and delivered in the donor's lifetime; or•deathbed gifts (gift causa mortis, donatio mortis causa) - a future gift made in expectation of the donor's imminent death.
Hong	The Hongs were major business houses in Canton, China and later Hong Kong with significant influence on patterns of consumerism, trade, manufacturing and other key areas of the economy. They were originally led by Howqua as head of the cohong.
Economic growth	Economic growth is the increase in the market value of the goods and services produced by an economy over time. It is conventionally measured as the percent rate of increase in real gross domestic product, or real GDP. Of more importance is the growth of the ratio of GDP to population (GDP per capita), which is also called per capita income. An increase in per capita income is referred to as intensive growth.
Nature	Nature is a concept with two major sets of inter-related meanings, referring on the one hand to the things which are natural, or subject to the normal working of 'laws of nature', or on the other hand to the essential properties and causes of those things to be what they naturally are, or in other words the laws of nature themselves.

17. Potential GDP and Economic Growth,

CHAPTER HIGHLIGHTS & NOTES: KEY TERMS, PEOPLE, PLACES, CONCEPTS

	How to understand the meaning and significance of nature has been a consistent theme of discussion within the history of Western Civilization, in the philosophical fields of metaphysics and epistemology, as well as in theology and science. The study of natural things and the regular laws which seem to govern them, as opposed to discussion about what it means to be natural, is the area of natural science.
Diminishing returns	In economics, diminishing returns is the decrease in the marginal (per-unit) output of a production process as the amount of a single factor of production is increased, while the amounts of all other factors of production stay constant. The law of diminishing returns states that in all productive processes, adding more of one factor of production, while holding all others constant ('ceteris paribus'), will at some point yield lower per-unit returns. The law of diminishing returns does not imply that adding more of a factor will decrease the total production, a condition known as negative returns, though in fact this is common.
Production function	In economics, a production function relates physical output of a production process to physical inputs or factors of production. The production function is one of the key concepts of mainstream neoclassical theories, used to define marginal product and to distinguish allocative efficiency, the defining focus of economics. The primary purpose of the production function is to address allocative efficiency in the use of factor inputs in production and the resulting distribution of income to those factors, while abstracting away from the technological problems of achieving technical efficiency, as an engineer or professional manager might understand it.
Demand	In economics, demand for a good or service is an entire listing of the quantity of the good or service that a market would choose to buy, for every possible market price of the good or service. (Note: This distinguishes 'demand' from 'quantity demanded', where demand is a listing or graphing of quantity demanded at each possible price. In contrast to demand, quantity demanded is the exact quantity demanded at a certain price.
Labor force	The labor force is the actual number of people available for work. The labor force of a country includes both the employed and the unemployed. The labor force participation rate, LFPR (or economic activity rate, EAR), is the ratio between the labor force and the overall size of their cohort (national population of the same age range).
Supply	In economics, supply refers to the amount of a product that producers and firms are willing to sell at a given price all other factors being held constant. Usually, supply is plotted as a supply curve showing the relationship of price to the amount of product businesses are willing to sell.
Labor market	Labor economics seeks to understand the functioning and dynamics of the markets for wage labor. Labor markets or job markets function through the interaction of workers and employers.

17. Potential GDP and Economic Growth,

CHAPTER HIGHLIGHTS & NOTES: KEY TERMS, PEOPLE, PLACES, CONCEPTS

Real wage	The term real wages refers to wages that have been adjusted for inflation, or, equivalently, wages in terms of the amount of goods and services that can be bought. This term is used in contrast to nominal wages or unadjusted wages. Because it has been adjusted to account for changes in the prices of goods and services, real wages provide a clearer representation of an individual's wages in terms of what they can afford to buy with those wages - specifically, in terms of the amount of goods and services that can be bought.
Participation	In finance, 'participation' is an ownership interest in a mortgage or other loan. In particular, loan participation is a cooperation of multiple lenders to issue a loan (known as participation loan) to one borrower. This is usually done in order to reduce individual risks of the lenders.
Full employment	Full employment, in macroeconomics, is the level of employment rates where there is no cyclical or deficient-demand unemployment. It is defined by the majority of mainstream economists as being an acceptable level of unemployment somewhere above 0%. The discrepancy from 0% arises due to non-cyclical types of unemployment.
Unemployment	Unemployment occurs when people are without work and actively seeking work. The unemployment rate is a measure of the prevalence of unemployment and it is calculated as a percentage by dividing the number of unemployed individuals by all individuals currently in the labor force. During periods of recession, an economy usually experiences a relatively high unemployment rate.
Productivity	Productivity is the ratio of output to inputs in production; it is an average measure of the efficiency of production. Efficiency of production means production's capability to create incomes which is measured by the formula real output value minus real input value. Increasing national productivity can raise living standards because more real income improves people's ability to purchase goods and services, enjoy leisure, improve housing and education and contribute to social and environmental programs.
Rate	In mathematics, a rate is a ratio between two measurements with different units. If the unit or quantity in respect of which something is changing is not specified, usually the rate is per unit time. However, a rate of change can be specified per unit time, or per unit of length or mass or another quantity.
Real GDP	Real Gross Domestic Product (real GDP) is a macroeconomic measure of the value of economic output adjusted for price changes . This adjustment transforms the money-value measure, nominal GDP, into an index for quantity of total output. GDP is the sum of consumer Spending, Investment made by industry, Excess of Exports over Imports and Government Spending.
Standard of living	Standard of living refers to the level of wealth, comfort, material goods and necessities available to a certain socioeconomic class in a certain geographic area.

17. Potential GDP and Economic Growth,

CHAPTER HIGHLIGHTS & NOTES: KEY TERMS, PEOPLE, PLACES, CONCEPTS

	The standard of living includes factors such as income, quality and availability of employment, class disparity, poverty rate, quality and affordability of housing, hours of work required to purchase necessities, gross domestic product, inflation rate, number of holiday days per year, affordable (or free) access to quality healthcare, quality and availability of education, life expectancy, incidence of disease, cost of goods and services, infrastructure, national economic growth, economic and political and stability, political and religious freedom, environmental quality, climate and safety. The standard of living is closely related to quality of life.
Bradford	Bradford lies at the heart of the City of Bradford, a metropolitan borough of West Yorkshire, in Northern England. It is situated in the foothills of the Pennines, 8.6 miles (14 km) west of Leeds, and 16 miles (26 km) northwest of Wakefield. Bradford became a municipal borough in 1847, and received its charter as a city in 1897. Following local government reform in 1974, city status was bestowed upon the wider metropolitan borough.
Industrial Revolution	The Industrial Revolution was the transition to new manufacturing processes in the period from about 1760 to sometime between 1820 and 1840. This transition included going from hand production methods to machines, new chemical manufacturing and iron production processes, improved efficiency of water power, the increasing use of steam power and the development of machine tools. It also included the change from wood and other bio-fuels to coal. Textiles were the dominant industry of the Industrial Revolution in terms of employment, value of output and capital invested.
Executive officer	An executive officer is generally a person responsible for running an organization, although the exact nature of the role varies depending on the organization.
Investment	Investment is time, energy, or matter spent in the hope of future benefits. Investment has different meanings in economics and finance. In economics, investment is the accumulation of newly produced physical entities, such as factories, machinery, houses, and goods inventories.
Saving	Precautionary savings occurs in response to uncertainty regarding future income. The precautionary motive to delay consumption and save in the current period rises due to the lack of completeness of insurance markets. Accordingly, individuals will not be able to insure against some bad state of the economy in the future.
Economic policy	Economic policy refers to the actions that governments take in the economic field. It covers the systems for setting interest rates and government budget as well as the labor market, national ownership, and many other areas of government interventions into the economy.

17. Potential GDP and Economic Growth,

CHAPTER HIGHLIGHTS & NOTES: KEY TERMS, PEOPLE, PLACES, CONCEPTS

Human capital	Human capital is the stock of knowledge, habits, social and personality attributes, including creativity, embodied in the ability to perform labor so as to produce economic value.
	Alternatively, Human capital is a collection of resources--all the knowledge, talents, skills, abilities, experience, intelligence, training, judgment, and wisdom possessed individually and collectively by individuals in a population.
Information revolution	The term information revolution describes current economic, social and technological trends beyond the Industrial Revolution.
	Many competing terms have been proposed that focus on different aspects of this societal development. The British polymath crystallographer J. D. Bernal (1939) introduced the term 'scientific and technical revolution' in his book The Social Function of Science to describe the new role that science and technology are coming to play within society.
Sources	Sources is a web portal for journalists, freelance writers, editors, authors and researchers, focusing especially on human sources: experts and spokespersons who are prepared to answer reporters' questions or make themselves available for on-air interviews.
Information Age	The Information Age is a period in human history characterized by the shift from traditional industry that the industrial revolution brought through industrialization, to an economy based on information computerization. The onset of the Information Age is associated with the Digital Revolution, just as the Industrial Revolution marked the onset of the Industrial Age.
	During the information age, the phenomenon is that the digital industry creates a knowledge-based society surrounded by a high-tech global economy that spans over its influence on how the manufacturing throughput and the service sector operate in an efficient and convenient way.
Internet	The Internet is a global system of interconnected computer networks that use the standard Internet protocol suite to link several billion devices worldwide. It is a network of networks that consists of millions of private, public, academic, business, and government networks, of local to global scope, that are linked by a broad array of electronic, wireless, and optical networking technologies. The Internet carries an extensive range of information resources and services, such as the inter-linked hypertext documents and applications of the World Wide Web (WWW), the infrastructure to support email, and peer-to-peer networks for file sharing and telephony.
Advance	Advance is a certified, independent trade union affiliated to the TUC representing workers within the bank Santander UK, the UK subsidiary of Santander Group. The union was formerly known as The Abbey National Group Union (ANGU) before it expanded to include staff of Alliance & Leicester and Bradford & Bingley following their acquisitions by Santander. Its aims are the supporting and representing its members in all aspects of their employment.

17. Potential GDP and Economic Growth,

CHAPTER HIGHLIGHTS & NOTES: KEY TERMS, PEOPLE, PLACES, CONCEPTS

Consumer	A consumer is a person or group of people, such as a household, who are the final users of products or services. The consumer's use is final in the sense that the product is usually not improved by the use.
Economic freedom	Economic freedom or economic liberty or right to economic liberty denotes the ability of members of a society to undertake economic direction and actions. This is a term used in economic and policy debates as well as a politicoeconomic philosophy. As with freedom generally, there are various definitions, but no universally accepted concept of economic freedom.
Property rights	Property rights are theoretical constructs in economics for determining how a resource is used and owned. Resources can be owned (the subject of property) by individuals, associations or governments. Property rights can be viewed as an attribute of an economic good.
Market	A market is one of the many varieties of systems, institutions, procedures, social relations and infrastructures whereby parties engage in exchange. While parties may exchange goods and services by barter, most markets rely on sellers offering their goods or services (including labor) in exchange for money from buyers. It can be said that a market is the process by which the prices of goods and services are established.
Circular flow	In economics, the terms circular flow of income or circular flow refer to a simple economic model which describes the reciprocal circulation of income between producers and consumers. In the circular flow model, the inter-dependent entities of producer and consumer are referred to as 'firms' and 'households' respectively and provide each other with factors in order to facilitate the flow of income. Firms provide consumers with goods and services in exchange for consumer expenditure and 'factors of production' from households.
International trade	International trade is the exchange of capital, goods, and services across international borders or territories. In most countries, such trade represents a significant share of gross domestic product (GDP). While international trade has been present throughout much of history, its economic, social, and political importance has been on the rise in recent centuries.
Outsourcing	In business, outsourcing is the contracting out of a business process to a third-party. The term 'outsourcing' became popular in the United States near the turn of the 21st century. Outsourcing sometimes involves transferring employees and assets from one firm to another, but not always.
Quality	Quality in business, engineering and manufacturing has a pragmatic interpretation as the non-inferiority or superiority of something; it is also defined as fitness for purpose. Quality is a perceptual, conditional, and somewhat subjective attribute and may be understood differently by different people. Consumers may focus on the specification quality of a product/service, or how it compares to competitors in the marketplace.
Trade	Trade, also called goods exchange economy, is to transfer the ownership of goods from one person or entity to another by getting a product or service in exchange from the buyer.

17. Potential GDP and Economic Growth,

CHAPTER HIGHLIGHTS & NOTES: KEY TERMS, PEOPLE, PLACES, CONCEPTS

Trade is sometimes loosely called commerce or financial transaction or barter. A network that allows trade is called a market.

CHAPTER QUIZ: KEY TERMS, PEOPLE, PLACES, CONCEPTS

1. _____ is an economic system in which trade, industry and the means of production are controlled by private owners with the goal of making profits in a market economy. Central characteristics of _____ include capital accumulation, competitive markets and wage labor. In a capitalist economy, the parties to a transaction typically determine the prices at which assets, goods, and services are exchanged.

   a. Cigar Box Method
   b. Cash crop
   c. Casa grande
   d. Capitalism

2. _____ is a relationship between two parties, usually based on a contract, one being the employer and the other being the employee.

   a. Fuel protests in the United Kingdom
   b. Battle of Annaberg
   c. Freikorps Lichtschlag
   d. Employment

3. In economics, _____ refers to the amount of a product that producers and firms are willing to sell at a given price all other factors being held constant. Usually, _____ is plotted as a _____ curve showing the relationship of price to the amount of product businesses are willing to sell.

   a. Base period
   b. Supply
   c. Blanket order
   d. Bond

4. . In economics, _____ are the inputs to the production process. Finished goods are the output. Input determines the quantity of output i.e. output depends upon input.

   a. Factors of production
   b. Bliss point
   c. Club good

17. Potential GDP and Economic Growth,

CHAPTER QUIZ: KEY TERMS, PEOPLE, PLACES, CONCEPTS

5. Precautionary _____s occurs in response to uncertainty regarding future income. The precautionary motive to delay consumption and save in the current period rises due to the lack of completeness of insurance markets. Accordingly, individuals will not be able to insure against some bad state of the economy in the future.

   a. Discount function
   b. Saving
   c. Cash crop
   d. Casa grande

ANSWER KEY
17. Potential GDP and Economic Growth,

1. d
2. d
3. b
4. a
5. b

You can take the complete Online Interactive Chapter Practice Test

for 17. Potential GDP and Economic Growth,
on all key terms, persons, places, and concepts.

No Additional Costs

http://www.Cram101.com

Register, send an email request to Travis.Reese@Cram101.com to get your user Id and password.

Include your customer order number, and ISBN number from your studyguide Retailer.

18. Money and the Monetary System,

CHAPTER OUTLINE: KEY TERMS, PEOPLE, PLACES, CONCEPTS

- Mean
- Money
- Good
- Goods and services
- Service
- Barter
- Medium of exchange
- Store of value
- Unit of account
- Currency
- Deposit
- Fiat money
- Debit card
- Commercial bank
- Federal Reserve
- Federal Reserve System
- Bank
- Profit
- Required reserve ratio
- Reserve
- Risk

18. Money and the Monetary System,
CHAPTER OUTLINE: KEY TERMS, PEOPLE, PLACES, CONCEPTS

_____	Federal funds
_____	Federal funds rate
_____	Net worth
_____	Asset
_____	Loan
_____	Credit union
_____	Financial capital
_____	Money market
_____	Money market fund
_____	Saving
_____	Savings and loan association
_____	Savings bank
_____	Capital
_____	Crisis
_____	Financial crisis
_____	Institution
_____	Rate
_____	Central bank
_____	Policy
_____	Reserve ratio
_____	Monetary base

18. Money and the Monetary System,

CHAPTER OUTLINE: KEY TERMS, PEOPLE, PLACES, CONCEPTS

	Open market
	Open market operation
	Quantitative easing
	Excess reserves
	Consumer
	Multiplier
	Money multiplier
	Bernanke
	Depression
	Great Depression
	Money creation

CHAPTER HIGHLIGHTS & NOTES: KEY TERMS, PEOPLE, PLACES, CONCEPTS

Mean — In mathematics, mean has several different definitions depending on the context.

In probability and statistics, mean and expected value are used synonymously to refer to one measure of the central tendency either of a probability distribution or of the random variable characterized by that distribution. In the case of a discrete probability distribution of a random variable X, the mean is equal to the sum over every possible value weighted by the probability of that value; that is, it is computed by taking the product of each possible value x of X and its probability P(x), and then adding all these products together, giving $\mu = \sum xP(x)$.

Money — Monetary disequilibrium theory is basically a product of the Monetarist school mainly represented in the works of Leland Yeager and Austrian macroeconomics.

18. Money and the Monetary System,

CHAPTER HIGHLIGHTS & NOTES: KEY TERMS, PEOPLE, PLACES, CONCEPTS

	The basic concept of monetary equilibrium (disequilibrium) was, however, defined in terms of an individual's demand for cash balance by Mises (1912) in his Theory of Money and Credit.
	Monetary Disequilibrium is one of three theories of macroeconomic fluctuations which accord an important role to money, the others being the Austrian theory of the business cycle and one based on rational expectations.
Good	In economics, a good is a material that satisfies human wants and provides utility, for example, to a consumer making a purchase. A common distinction is made between 'goods' that are tangible property (also called goods) and services, which are non-physical. Commodities may be used as a synonym for economic goods but often refer to marketable raw materials and primary products.
Goods and services	In economics, goods and services are the outcome of human efforts to meet the wants and needs of people. Economic output is divided into physical goods and intangible services. Goods are items that can be seen and touched, such as books, pens, salt, shoes, hats, and folders.
Service	In economics, a service is an intangible commodity. That is, services are an example of intangible economic goods.
	Service provision is often an economic activity where the buyer does not generally, except by exclusive contract, obtain exclusive ownership of the thing purchased.
Barter	Barter is a system of exchange by which goods or services are directly exchanged for other goods or services without using a medium of exchange, such as money. It is distinguishable from gift economies in that the reciprocal exchange is immediate and not delayed in time. It is usually bilateral, but may be multilateral (i.e., mediated through barter organizations) and usually exists parallel to monetary systems in most developed countries, though to a very limited extent.
Medium of exchange	A medium of exchange is an intermediary used in trade to avoid the inconveniences of a pure barter system.
	By contrast, as William Stanley Jevons argued, in a barter system there must be a coincidence of wants before two people can trade - one must want exactly what the other has to offer, when and where it is offered, so that the exchange can occur. A medium of exchange permits the value of goods to be assessed and rendered in terms of the intermediary, most often, a form of money widely accepted to buy any other good.
Store of value	A store of value is the function of an asset that can be saved, retrieved and exchanged at a later time, and be predictably useful when retrieved. The most common store of value in modern times has been money, currency, or a commodity like gold, or financial capital. The point of any store of value is intrinsic risk management due to an inherent stable demand for the underlying asset.

18. Money and the Monetary System,

CHAPTER HIGHLIGHTS & NOTES: KEY TERMS, PEOPLE, PLACES, CONCEPTS

Unit of account	The Unidad de Fomento is a Unit of account that is used in Chile. The exchange rate between the UF and the Chilean peso is now (today) constantly adjusted to inflation so that the value of the Unidad de Fomento remains constant on a daily basis during low inflation.
	It was created on January 20, 1968, for the use in determining principal (monetary item) and interest (constant real value non-monetary item) in international secured loans (monetary items) for development, subject to revaluation according to the variations of inflation.
Currency	A currency in the most specific use of the word refers to money in any form when in actual use or circulation, as a medium of exchange, especially circulating paper money. This use is synonymous with banknotes, or (sometimes) with banknotes plus coins, meaning the physical tokens used for money by a government.
	A much more general use of the word currency is anything that is used in any circumstances, as a medium of exchange.
Deposit	Individuals and corporations need money to pursue their daily business. They place the money on deposit to earn interest, using the money market. Types of deposits are:•Transactional account (checking account or current account, by country), the depositor has the right to use the money at any time, sometimes short notice periods are agreed; also called call deposit or sight deposit•Term deposit bear a fixed time and fixed interest rate•Fixed deposit in India•Overnight lending occurs usually from noon to noon, using a special rate.
Fiat money	Fiat money is money that derives its value from government regulation or law. The term fiat currency is used when a fiat money is used as the main currency of the country. The term derives from the Latin fiat ('let it be done', 'it shall be').
Debit card	A debit card is a plastic payment card that provides the cardholder electronic access to his or her bank account(s) at a financial institution. Some cards have a stored value with which a payment is made, while most relay a message to the cardholder's bank to withdraw funds from a payer's designated bank account. The card, where accepted, can be used instead of cash when making purchases.
Commercial bank	A commercial bank is a type of bank that provides services such as accepting deposits, making business loans, and offering basic investment products.
	Commercial bank can also refer to a bank or a division of a bank that mostly deals with deposits and loans from corporations or large businesses, as opposed to individual members of the public.
	In the US the term commercial bank was often used to distinguish it from an investment bank due to differences in bank regulation.

18. Money and the Monetary System,

CHAPTER HIGHLIGHTS & NOTES: KEY TERMS, PEOPLE, PLACES, CONCEPTS

Federal Reserve	The Federal Reserve System (also known as the Federal Reserve, and informally as the Fed) is the central banking system of the United States. It was created on December 23, 1913, with the enactment of the Federal Reserve Act, largely in response to a series of financial panics, particularly a severe panic in 1907. Over time, the roles and responsibilities of the Federal Reserve System have expanded, and its structure has evolved. Events such as the Great Depression were major factors leading to changes in the system.
Federal Reserve System	The Federal Reserve System is the central banking system of the United States. It was created on December 23, 1913, with the enactment of the Federal Reserve Act, largely in response to a series of financial panics, particularly a severe panic in 1907. Over time, the roles and responsibilities of the Federal Reserve System have expanded, and its structure has evolved. Events such as the Great Depression were major factors leading to changes in the system.
Bank	A bank is a financial institution and a financial intermediary that accepts deposits and channels those deposits into lending activities, either directly by loaning or indirectly through capital markets. A bank links together customers that have capital deficits and customers with capital surpluses. Due to their influential status within the financial system and upon national economies, banks are highly regulated in most countries.
Profit	In neoclassical microeconomic theory, the term profit has two related but distinct meanings. Economic profit is similar to accounting profit but smaller because it reflects the total opportunity costs (both explicit and implicit) of a venture to an investor. Normal profit refers to a situation in which the economic profit is zero.
Required reserve ratio	The reserve requirement is a central bank regulation employed by most, but not all, of the world's central banks, that sets the minimum fraction of customer deposits and notes that each commercial bank must hold as reserves (rather than lend out). These required reserves are normally in the form of cash stored physically in a bank vault (vault cash) or deposits made with a central bank. The required reserve ratio is sometimes used as a tool in monetary policy, influencing the country's borrowing and interest rates by changing the amount of funds available for banks to make loans with.
Reserve	In financial accounting, the term reserve is most commonly used to describe any part of shareholders' equity, except for basic share capital. In nonprofit accounting, an 'operating reserve' is commonly used to refer to unrestricted cash on hand available to sustain an organization, and nonprofit boards usually specify a target of maintaining several months of operating cash or a percentage of their annual income, called an Operating Reserve Ratio.

18. Money and the Monetary System,

CHAPTER HIGHLIGHTS & NOTES: KEY TERMS, PEOPLE, PLACES, CONCEPTS

Risk	Risk is the potential of losing something of value, weighed against the potential to gain something of value. Values (such as physical health, social status, emotional well being or financial wealth) can be gained or lost when taking risk resulting from a given action, activity and/or inaction, foreseen or unforeseen. Risk can also be defined as the intentional interaction with uncertainty.
Federal funds	In the United States, federal funds are overnight borrowings between banks and other entities to maintain their bank reserves at the Federal Reserve. Banks keep reserves at Federal Reserve Banks to meet their reserve requirements and to clear financial transactions. Transactions in the federal funds market enable depository institutions with reserve balances in excess of reserve requirements to lend reserves to institutions with reserve deficiencies.
Federal funds rate	In the United States, the federal funds rate is the interest rate at which depository institutions actively trade balances held at the Federal Reserve, called federal funds, with each other, usually overnight, on an uncollateralized basis. Institutions with surplus balances in their accounts lend those balances to institutions in need of larger balances. The federal funds rate is an important benchmark in financial markets.
Net worth	A millionaire is an individual whose net worth or wealth is equal to or exceeds one million units of currency. It can also be a person who owns one million units of currency in a bank account or savings account. Depending on the currency, a certain level of prestige is associated with being a millionaire, which makes that amount of wealth a goal for some, and almost unattainable for others.
Asset	An 'asset' in economic theory is an output good which can only be partially consumed or input as a factor of production (like a cement mixer) which can only be partially used up in production. The necessary quality for an asset is that value remains after the period of analysis so it can be used as a store of value. As such, financial instruments like corporate bonds and common stocks are assets because they store value for the next period.
Loan	An introductory rate is an interest rate charged to a customer during the initial stages of a loan. The rate, which can be as low as 0%, is not permanent and after it expires a normal or higher than normal rate will apply. The purpose of the introductory rate is to market the loan to customers and to seem attractive.
Credit union	A credit union is a member-owned financial cooperative, democratically controlled by its members, and operated for the purpose of promoting thrift, providing credit at competitive rates, and providing other financial services to its members. Many credit unions also provide services intended to support community development or sustainable international development on a local level.

18. Money and the Monetary System,

CHAPTER HIGHLIGHTS & NOTES: KEY TERMS, PEOPLE, PLACES, CONCEPTS

Financial capital	Financial capital is money used by entrepreneurs and businesses to buy what they need to make their products or to provide their services to the sector of the economy upon which their operation is based, i.e. retail, corporate, investment banking, etc.
Money market	As money became a commodity, the money market became a component of the financial markets for assets involved in short-term borrowing, lending, buying and selling with original maturities of one year or less. Trading in the money markets is done over the counter and is wholesale. Various instruments exist, such as Treasury bills, commercial paper, bankers' acceptances, deposits, certificates of deposit, bills of exchange, repurchase agreements, federal funds, and short-lived mortgage-, and asset-backed securities.
Money market fund	A money market fund is an open-ended mutual fund that invests in short-term debt securities such as US Treasury bills and commercial paper. Money market funds are widely (though not necessarily accurately) regarded as being as safe as bank deposits yet providing a higher yield. Regulated in the US under the Investment Company Act of 1940, money market funds are important providers of liquidity to financial intermediaries.
Saving	Precautionary savings occurs in response to uncertainty regarding future income. The precautionary motive to delay consumption and save in the current period rises due to the lack of completeness of insurance markets. Accordingly, individuals will not be able to insure against some bad state of the economy in the future.
Savings and loan association	A savings and loan association, also known as a thrift, is a financial institution that specializes in accepting savings deposits and making mortgage and other loans. The terms 'S&L' or 'thrift' are mainly used in the United States; similar institutions in the United Kingdom, Ireland and some Commonwealth countries include building societies and trustee savings banks. They are often mutually held (often called mutual savings banks), meaning that the depositors and borrowers are members with voting rights, and have the ability to direct the financial and managerial goals of the organization like the members of a credit union or the policyholders of a mutual insurance company.
Savings bank	A savings bank is a financial institution whose primary purpose is accepting savings deposits and paying interest on those deposits. They originated in Europe during the 18th century with the aim of providing access to savings products to all levels in the population. Often associated with social good these early banks were often designed to encourage low income people to save money and have access to banking services.
Capital	In economics, capital goods, real capital, or capital assets are already-produced durable goods or any non-financial asset that is used in production of goods or services.

18. Money and the Monetary System,

CHAPTER HIGHLIGHTS & NOTES: KEY TERMS, PEOPLE, PLACES, CONCEPTS

	Capital goods are not significantly consumed in the production process though they may depreciate. How a capital good or is maintained or returned to its pre-production state varies with the type of capital involved.
Crisis	A crisis is any event that is, or is expected to lead to, an unstable and dangerous situation affecting an individual, group, community, or whole society. Crises are deemed to be negative changes in the security, economic, political, societal, or environmental affairs, especially when they occur abruptly, with little or no warning. More loosely, it is a term meaning 'a testing time' or an 'emergency event'.
Financial crisis	The term financial crisis is applied broadly to a variety of situations in which some financial assets suddenly lose a large part of their nominal value. In the 19th and early 20th centuries, many financial crises were associated with banking panics, and many recessions coincided with these panics. Other situations that are often called financial crises include stock market crashes and the bursting of other financial bubbles, currency crises, and sovereign defaults.
Institution	An institution is any structure or mechanism of social order governing the behaviour of a set of individuals within a given community; may it be human or a specific animal one. Institutions are identified with a social purpose, transcending individuals and intentions by mediating the rules that govern living behavior. The term 'institution' is commonly applied to customs and behavior patterns important to a society, as well as to particular formal organizations of government and public services.
Rate	In mathematics, a rate is a ratio between two measurements with different units. If the unit or quantity in respect of which something is changing is not specified, usually the rate is per unit time. However, a rate of change can be specified per unit time, or per unit of length or mass or another quantity.
Central bank	A central bank, reserve bank, or monetary authority is an institution that manages a state's currency, money supply, and interest rates. Central banks also usually oversee the commercial banking system of their respective countries. In contrast to a commercial bank, a central bank possesses a monopoly on increasing the amount of money in the nation, and usually also prints the national currency, which usually serves as the nation's legal tender.
Policy	A policy is a principle or protocol to guide decisions and achieve rational outcomes. A policy is a statement of intent, and is implemented as a procedure or protocol. Policies are generally adopted by the Board of or senior governance body within an organization whereas procedures or protocols would be developed and adopted by senior executive officers.

18. Money and the Monetary System,

CHAPTER HIGHLIGHTS & NOTES: KEY TERMS, PEOPLE, PLACES, CONCEPTS

Reserve ratio	The reserve requirement (or cash reserve ratio) is a central bank regulation employed by most, but not all, of the world's central banks, that sets the minimum fraction of customer deposits and notes that each commercial bank must hold as reserves. These required reserves are normally in the form of cash stored physically in a bank vault (vault cash) or deposits made with a central bank.
	The required reserve ratio is sometimes used as a tool in monetary policy, influencing the country's borrowing and interest rates by changing the amount of funds available for banks to make loans with.
Monetary base	In economics, the monetary base in a country is defined as the portion of the commercial banks' reserves that are maintained in accounts with their central bank plus the total currency circulating in the public (which includes the currency, also known as vault cash, that is physically held in the banks' vault).
	The monetary base should not be confused with the money supply which consists of the total currency circulating in the public plus the non-bank deposits with commercial banks.
Open market	The term open market is used generally to refer to a situation close to free trade and in a more specific technical sense to interbank trade in securities. In principle, a fully open market is a completely free market in which all economic actors can trade without any external constraint.
Open market operation	An open market operation is an activity by a central bank to buy or sell government bonds on the open market. A central bank uses them as the primary means of implementing monetary policy. The usual aim of open market operations is to manipulate the short term interest rate and the supply of base money in an economy, and thus indirectly control the total money supply, in effect expanding money or contracting the money supply.
Quantitative easing	Quantitative easing is an unconventional monetary policy used by central banks to stimulate the economy when standard monetary policy has become ineffective. A central bank implements quantitative easing by buying specified amounts of financial assets from commercial banks and other private institutions, thus increasing the monetary base and lowering the yield on those financial assets. This is distinguished from the more usual policy of buying or selling short term government bonds in order to keep interbank interest rates at a specified target value.
Excess reserves	In banking, excess reserves are bank reserves in excess of a reserve requirement set by a central bank. They are reserves of cash more than the required amounts.
	In the United States, bank reserves are held as FRB (Federal Reserve Bank) credit in FRB accounts; they are not separated into separate 'minimum reserves' and 'excess reserves' accounts.
Consumer	A consumer is a person or group of people, such as a household, who are the final users of products or services.

18. Money and the Monetary System,

CHAPTER HIGHLIGHTS & NOTES: KEY TERMS, PEOPLE, PLACES, CONCEPTS

	The consumer's use is final in the sense that the product is usually not improved by the use.
Multiplier	In economics, a multiplier is a factor of proportionality that measures how much an endogenous variable changes in response to a change in some exogenous variable. For example, suppose variable x changes by 1 unit, which causes another variable y to change by M units. Then the multiplier is M.
Money multiplier	In monetary economics, a money multiplier is one of various closely related ratios of commercial bank money to central bank money under a fractional-reserve banking system. Most often, it measures the maximum amount of commercial bank money that can be created by a given unit of central bank money. That is, in a fractional-reserve banking system, the total amount of loans that commercial banks are allowed to extend (the commercial bank money that they can legally create) is a multiple of reserves; this multiple is the reciprocal of the reserve ratio, and it is an economic multiplier.
Bernanke	Ben Shalom Bernanke is an American economist at the Brookings Institution who served two terms as chairman of the Federal Reserve, the central bank of the United States from 2006 to 2014. During his tenure as chairman, Bernanke oversaw the Federal Reserve's response to the late-2000s financial crisis. Before becoming Federal Reserve chairman, Bernanke was a tenured professor at Princeton University and chaired the department of economics there from 1996 to September 2002, when he went on public service leave. From 2002 until 2005, he was a member of the Board of Governors of the Federal Reserve System, proposed the Bernanke Doctrine, and first discussed 'the Great Moderation' -- the theory that traditional business cycles have declined in volatility in recent decades through structural changes that have occurred in the international economy, particularly increases in the economic stability of developing nations, diminishing the influence of macroeconomic (monetary and fiscal) policy.
Depression	In economics, a depression is a sustained, long-term downturn in economic activity in one or more economies. It is a more severe downturn than a recession, which is seen by some economists as inevitable part of capitalist economy. Considered by some economists to be a rare and extreme form of recession, a depression is characterized by its length; by abnormally large increases in unemployment; falls in the availability of credit, often due to some kind of banking or financial crisis; shrinking output as buyers dry up and suppliers cut back on production and investment; large number of bankruptcies including sovereign debt defaults; significantly reduced amounts of trade and commerce, especially international; as well as highly volatile relative currency value fluctuations, most often due to devaluations.

18. Money and the Monetary System,

CHAPTER HIGHLIGHTS & NOTES: KEY TERMS, PEOPLE, PLACES, CONCEPTS

Great Depression	The Great Depression was a severe worldwide economic depression in the decade preceding World War II. The timing of the Great Depression varied across nations, but in most countries it started in 1930 and lasted until the late 1930s or middle 1940s. It was the longest, deepest, and most widespread depression of the 20th century. In the 21st century, the Great Depression is commonly used as an example of how far the world's economy can decline.
Money creation	In economics, money creation is the process by which the money supply of a country or a monetary region is increased. A central bank may introduce new money into the economy (termed 'expansionary monetary policy') by purchasing financial assets or lending money to financial institutions. Commercial bank lending also creates money under the form of demand deposits).

CHAPTER QUIZ: KEY TERMS, PEOPLE, PLACES, CONCEPTS

1. In mathematics, _____ has several different definitions depending on the context.

    In probability and statistics, _____ and expected value are used synonymously to refer to one measure of the central tendency either of a probability distribution or of the random variable characterized by that distribution. In the case of a discrete probability distribution of a random variable X, the _____ is equal to the sum over every possible value weighted by the probability of that value; that is, it is computed by taking the product of each possible value x of X and its probability P(x), and then adding all these products together, giving $\mu = \sum xP(x)$.

    a. Cause of death
    b. Ceiling effect
    c. Central limit theorem
    d. Mean

2. . Individuals and corporations need money to pursue their daily business. They place the money on _____ to earn interest, using the money market. Types of _____s are:•Transactional account (checking account or current account, by country), the depositor has the right to use the money at any time, sometimes short notice periods are agreed; also called call _____ or sight _____ •Term _____ bear a fixed time and fixed interest rate•Fixed _____ in India•Overnight lending occurs usually from noon to noon, using a special rate.

    a. 3-6-3 Rule
    b. Balance transfer
    c. Deposit

18. Money and the Monetary System,

CHAPTER QUIZ: KEY TERMS, PEOPLE, PLACES, CONCEPTS

3. In economics, a _____ is a factor of proportionality that measures how much an endogenous variable changes in response to a change in some exogenous variable.

   For example, suppose variable x changes by 1 unit, which causes another variable y to change by M units. Then the _____ is M.

   a. Boukaseff scale
   b. Multiplier
   c. Business cycle accounting
   d. Classical dichotomy

4. A _____ is a person or group of people, such as a household, who are the final users of products or services. The _____'s use is final in the sense that the product is usually not improved by the use.

   a. Consumer
   b. Budget constraint
   c. Budget set
   d. Complementary good

5. The reserve requirement is a central bank regulation employed by most, but not all, of the world's central banks, that sets the minimum fraction of customer deposits and notes that each commercial bank must hold as reserves (rather than lend out). These required reserves are normally in the form of cash stored physically in a bank vault (vault cash) or deposits made with a central bank.

   The _____ is sometimes used as a tool in monetary policy, influencing the country's borrowing and interest rates by changing the amount of funds available for banks to make loans with.

   a. Required reserve ratio
   b. Business valuation
   c. Business value
   d. Capital asset

ANSWER KEY
18. Money and the Monetary System,

1. d
2. c
3. b
4. a
5. a

You can take the complete Online Interactive Chapter Practice Test

for 18. Money and the Monetary System,
on all key terms, persons, places, and concepts.

No Additional Costs

http://www.Cram101.com

Register, send an email request to Travis.Reese@Cram101.com to get your user Id and password.

Include your customer order number, and ISBN number from your studyguide Retailer.

19. Aggregate Supply and Aggregate Demand,

CHAPTER OUTLINE: KEY TERMS, PEOPLE, PLACES, CONCEPTS

_____ Aggregate supply

_____ Labor force

_____ Market

_____ Market equilibrium

_____ Real GDP

_____ Demand

_____ Good

_____ Labor market

_____ Service

_____ Supply

_____ Real wage

_____ Rate

_____ Business cycle

_____ Price level

_____ Substitution bias

_____ Money

_____ Price

_____ Aggregate demand

_____ Interest rate

_____ Real interest rate

_____ Export

19. Aggregate Supply and Aggregate Demand,

CHAPTER OUTLINE: KEY TERMS, PEOPLE, PLACES, CONCEPTS

_____ Import

_____ Exchange rate

_____ Foreign exchange market

_____ Monetary policy

_____ World economy

_____ Circular flow

_____ Goods and services

_____ Multiplier

_____ Macroeconomic

_____ Full employment

_____ Inflationary gap

_____ Recessionary gap

_____ Gap

_____ Hong

_____ Inferior good

_____ Economic growth

_____ Trends

_____ Real business cycle

_____ Demand-pull inflation

_____ Inflation

_____ Cost-push inflation

19. Aggregate Supply and Aggregate Demand,
CHAPTER OUTLINE: KEY TERMS, PEOPLE, PLACES, CONCEPTS

	Stagflation
	Employment
	Great Depression
	Consumer
	Deflation
	Consumption
	Financial capital
	Recession
	Capital
	Crisis
	Economy
	Expenditure
	Financial crisis

19. Aggregate Supply and Aggregate Demand,

CHAPTER HIGHLIGHTS & NOTES: KEY TERMS, PEOPLE, PLACES, CONCEPTS

Aggregate supply	In economics, aggregate supply is the total supply of goods and services that firms in a national economy plan on selling during a specific time period. It is the total amount of goods and services that firms are willing to sell at a given price level in an economy.
Labor force	The labor force is the actual number of people available for work. The labor force of a country includes both the employed and the unemployed. The labor force participation rate, LFPR (or economic activity rate, EAR), is the ratio between the labor force and the overall size of their cohort (national population of the same age range).
Market	A market is one of the many varieties of systems, institutions, procedures, social relations and infrastructures whereby parties engage in exchange. While parties may exchange goods and services by barter, most markets rely on sellers offering their goods or services (including labor) in exchange for money from buyers. It can be said that a market is the process by which the prices of goods and services are established.
Market equilibrium	In economics, economic equilibrium is a state where economic forces such as supply and demand are balanced and in the absence of external influences the values of economic variables will not change. For example, in the standard text-book model of perfect competition, equilibrium occurs at the point at which quantity demanded and quantity supplied are equal. Market equilibrium in this case refers to a condition where a market price is established through competition such that the amount of goods or services sought by buyers is equal to the amount of goods or services produced by sellers.
Real GDP	Real Gross Domestic Product (real GDP) is a macroeconomic measure of the value of economic output adjusted for price changes . This adjustment transforms the money-value measure, nominal GDP, into an index for quantity of total output. GDP is the sum of consumer Spending, Investment made by industry, Excess of Exports over Imports and Government Spending.
Demand	In economics, demand for a good or service is an entire listing of the quantity of the good or service that a market would choose to buy, for every possible market price of the good or service. (Note: This distinguishes 'demand' from 'quantity demanded', where demand is a listing or graphing of quantity demanded at each possible price. In contrast to demand, quantity demanded is the exact quantity demanded at a certain price.
Good	In economics, a good is a material that satisfies human wants and provides utility, for example, to a consumer making a purchase. A common distinction is made between 'goods' that are tangible property (also called goods) and services, which are non-physical. Commodities may be used as a synonym for economic goods but often refer to marketable raw materials and primary products.
Labor market	Labor economics seeks to understand the functioning and dynamics of the markets for wage labor. Labor markets or job markets function through the interaction of workers and employers.

19. Aggregate Supply and Aggregate Demand,

CHAPTER HIGHLIGHTS & NOTES: KEY TERMS, PEOPLE, PLACES, CONCEPTS

Service	In economics, a service is an intangible commodity. That is, services are an example of intangible economic goods. Service provision is often an economic activity where the buyer does not generally, except by exclusive contract, obtain exclusive ownership of the thing purchased.
Supply	In economics, supply refers to the amount of a product that producers and firms are willing to sell at a given price all other factors being held constant. Usually, supply is plotted as a supply curve showing the relationship of price to the amount of product businesses are willing to sell.
Real wage	The term real wages refers to wages that have been adjusted for inflation, or, equivalently, wages in terms of the amount of goods and services that can be bought. This term is used in contrast to nominal wages or unadjusted wages. Because it has been adjusted to account for changes in the prices of goods and services, real wages provide a clearer representation of an individual's wages in terms of what they can afford to buy with those wages - specifically, in terms of the amount of goods and services that can be bought.
Rate	In mathematics, a rate is a ratio between two measurements with different units. If the unit or quantity in respect of which something is changing is not specified, usually the rate is per unit time. However, a rate of change can be specified per unit time, or per unit of length or mass or another quantity.
Business cycle	The term business cycle refers to economy-wide fluctuations in production, trade and economic activity in general over several months or years in an economy organized on free-enterprise principles. The business cycle is the upward and downward movements of levels of GDP (gross domestic product) and refers to the period of expansions and contractions in the level of economic activities (business fluctuations) around its long-term growth trend. These fluctuations occur around a long-term growth trend, and typically involve shifts over time between periods of relatively rapid economic growth (an expansion or boom), and periods of relative stagnation or decline (a contraction or recession).
Price level	The general price level is a hypothetical measure of overall prices for some set of goods and services, in a given region during a given interval, normalized relative to some base set. Typically, a price level is approximated with a price index.
Substitution bias	Substitution bias describes a bias in economics index numbers arising from tendency to purchase inexpensive substitutes for expensive items when prices change.

19. Aggregate Supply and Aggregate Demand,

CHAPTER HIGHLIGHTS & NOTES: KEY TERMS, PEOPLE, PLACES, CONCEPTS

	Substitution bias occurs when two or more items experience a change of price relative to each other. Consumers will consume more of the now comparatively inexpensive good and less of the now relatively more expensive good.
Money	Monetary disequilibrium theory is basically a product of the Monetarist school mainly represented in the works of Leland Yeager and Austrian macroeconomics. The basic concept of monetary equilibrium (disequilibrium) was, however, defined in terms of an individual's demand for cash balance by Mises (1912) in his Theory of Money and Credit.
	Monetary Disequilibrium is one of three theories of macroeconomic fluctuations which accord an important role to money, the others being the Austrian theory of the business cycle and one based on rational expectations.
Price	In ordinary usage, price is the quantity of payment or compensation given by one party to another in return for goods or services.
	In modern economies, prices are generally expressed in units of some form of currency. (For commodities, they are expressed as currency per unit weight of the commodity, e.g. euros per kilogram).
Aggregate demand	In economics, aggregate behavior refers to relationships between economic aggregates such as national income, government expenditure and aggregate demand. For example, the consumption function is a relationship between aggregate demand for consumption and aggregate disposable income.
	Models of aggregate behavior may be derived from direct observation of the economy, or from models of individual behavior.
Interest rate	An interest rate is the rate at which interest is paid by a borrower for the use of money that they borrow from a lender (creditor). Specifically, the interest rate is a percent of principal (P) paid a certain amount of times (m) per period (usually quoted per annum). For example, a small company borrows capital from a bank to buy new assets for its business, and in return the lender receives interest at a predetermined interest rate for deferring the use of funds and instead lending it to the borrower.
Real interest rate	The real interest rate is the rate of interest an investor expects to receive after allowing for inflation. It can be described more formally by the Fisher equation, which states that the real interest rate is approximately the nominal interest rate minus the inflation rate. If, for example, an investor were able to lock in a 5% interest rate for the coming year and anticipated a 2% rise in prices, they would expect to earn a real interest rate of 3%.

19. Aggregate Supply and Aggregate Demand,

CHAPTER HIGHLIGHTS & NOTES: KEY TERMS, PEOPLE, PLACES, CONCEPTS

Export	The term export means shipping the goods and services out of the port of a country. The seller of such goods and services is referred to as an 'exporter' who is based in the country of export whereas the overseas based buyer is referred to as an 'importer'. In International Trade, 'exports' refers to selling goods and services produced in the home country to other markets.
Import	An import is a good brought into a jurisdiction, especially across a national border, from an external source. The purchaser of the exotic good is called an importer. An import in the receiving country is an export from the sending country.
Exchange rate	European Monetary System was an arrangement established in 1979 under the Jenkins European Commission where most nations of the European Economic Community (EEC) linked their currencies to prevent large fluctuations relative to one another. After the demise of the Bretton Woods system in 1971, most of the EEC countries agreed in 1972 to maintain stable exchange rates by preventing exchange rate fluctuations of more than 2.25% (the European 'currency snake'). In March 1979, this system was replaced by the European Monetary System, and the European Currency Unit (ECU) was defined.
Foreign exchange market	The foreign exchange market is a global decentralized market for the trading of currencies. The main participants in this market are the larger international banks. Financial centers around the world function as anchors of trading between a wide range of multiple types of buyers and sellers around the clock, with the exception of weekends.
Monetary policy	Monetary policy is the process by which the monetary authority of a country controls the supply of money, often targeting a rate of interest for the purpose of promoting economic growth and stability. The official goals usually include relatively stable prices and low unemployment. Monetary economics provides insight into how to craft optimal monetary policy.
World economy	The world economy, or global economy, generally refers to the economy, which is based on economies of all of the world's countries' national economies. Also global economy can be seen as the economy of global society and national economies - as economies of local societies, making the global one. It can be evaluated in various kind of ways.
Circular flow	In economics, the terms circular flow of income or circular flow refer to a simple economic model which describes the reciprocal circulation of income between producers and consumers. In the circular flow model, the inter-dependent entities of producer and consumer are referred to as 'firms' and 'households' respectively and provide each other with factors in order to facilitate the flow of income. Firms provide consumers with goods and services in exchange for consumer expenditure and 'factors of production' from households.
Goods and services	In economics, goods and services are the outcome of human efforts to meet the wants and needs of people. Economic output is divided into physical goods and intangible services.

19. Aggregate Supply and Aggregate Demand,

CHAPTER HIGHLIGHTS & NOTES: KEY TERMS, PEOPLE, PLACES, CONCEPTS

Multiplier	In economics, a multiplier is a factor of proportionality that measures how much an endogenous variable changes in response to a change in some exogenous variable. For example, suppose variable x changes by 1 unit, which causes another variable y to change by M units. Then the multiplier is M.
Macroeconomic	Macroeconomics is a branch of economics dealing with the performance, structure, behavior, and decision-making of an economy as a whole, rather than individual markets. This includes national, regional, and global economies. With microeconomics, macroeconomics is one of the two most general fields in economics.
Full employment	Full employment, in macroeconomics, is the level of employment rates where there is no cyclical or deficient-demand unemployment. It is defined by the majority of mainstream economists as being an acceptable level of unemployment somewhere above 0%. The discrepancy from 0% arises due to non-cyclical types of unemployment.
Inflationary gap	An inflationary gap, in economics, is the amount by which the actual gross domestic product exceeds potential full-employment GDP. It is one type of output gap, the other being a recessionary gap.
Recessionary gap	The GDP gap or the output gap is the difference between actual GDP or actual output and potential GDP. The calculation for the output gap is Y-Y* where Y is actual output and Y* is potential output. If this calculation yields a positive number it is called an inflationary gap and indicates the growth of aggregate demand is outpacing the growth of aggregate supply--possibly creating inflation; if the calculation yields a negative number it is called a recessionary gap--possibly signifying deflation.
Gap	A gap is defined as an unfilled space or interval. On a technical analysis chart, a gap represents an area where no trading takes place. On the Japanese candlestick chart, a window is interpreted as a gap.
Hong	The Hongs were major business houses in Canton, China and later Hong Kong with significant influence on patterns of consumerism, trade, manufacturing and other key areas of the economy. They were originally led by Howqua as head of the cohong.
Inferior good	In economics, an inferior good is a good that decreases in demand when consumer income rises, unlike normal goods, for which the opposite is observed. Normal goods are those for which consumers' demand increases when their income increases. This would be the opposite of a superior good, one that is often associated with wealth and the wealthy, whereas an inferior good is often associated with lower socio-economic groups.
Economic growth	Economic growth is the increase in the market value of the goods and services produced by an economy over time. It is conventionally measured as the percent rate of increase in real gross domestic product, or real GDP.

19. Aggregate Supply and Aggregate Demand,
CHAPTER HIGHLIGHTS & NOTES: KEY TERMS, PEOPLE, PLACES, CONCEPTS

	Of more importance is the growth of the ratio of GDP to population (GDP per capita), which is also called per capita income. An increase in per capita income is referred to as intensive growth.
Trends	Trends is a society, philanthropy, fashion and lifestyle magazine published in Arizona. Created by Danny Medina in 1982, it was purchased by Bill Dougherty in 2001, who now serves as its publisher. Trends has a 501(c)(3) arm, the Trends Charitable Fund (TCF), which raises money for underserved women's and children's charitable organizations.
Real business cycle	Real business cycle theory are a class of New classical macroeconomics models in which business cycle fluctuations to a large extent can be accounted for by real (in contrast to nominal) shocks. Unlike other leading theories of the business cycle, Real business cycle theory sees business cycle fluctuations as the efficient response to exogenous changes in the real economic environment. That is, the level of national output necessarily maximizes expected utility, and government should therefore concentrate on long-run structural policy changes and not intervene through discretionary fiscal or monetary policy designed to actively smooth out economic short-term fluctuations.
Demand-pull inflation	Demand-pull inflation is asserted to arise when aggregate demand in an economy outpaces aggregate supply. It involves inflation rising as real gross domestic product rises and unemployment falls, as the economy moves along the Phillips curve. This is commonly described as 'too much money chasing too few goods'.
Inflation	In economics, inflation is a sustained increase in the general price level of goods and services in an economy over a period of time. When the general price level rises, each unit of currency buys fewer goods and services. Consequently, inflation reflects a reduction in the purchasing power per unit of money - a loss of real value in the medium of exchange and unit of account within the economy.
Cost-push inflation	Cost-push inflation is an alleged type of inflation caused by substantial increases in the cost of important goods or services where no suitable alternative is available. A situation that has been often cited of this was the oil crisis of the 1970s, which some economists see as a major cause of the inflation experienced in the Western world in that decade. It is argued that this inflation resulted from increases in the cost of petroleum imposed by the member states of OPEC. Since petroleum is so important to industrialised economies, a large increase in its price can lead to the increase in the price of most products, raising the inflation rate.
Stagflation	Stagflation, a portmanteau of stagnation and inflation, is a term used in economics to describe a situation where the inflation rate is high, the economic growth rate slows down, and unemployment remains steadily high. It raises a dilemma for economic policy since actions designed to lower inflation may exacerbate unemployment, and vice versa.

19. Aggregate Supply and Aggregate Demand,

CHAPTER HIGHLIGHTS & NOTES: KEY TERMS, PEOPLE, PLACES, CONCEPTS

	The term is generally attributed to a British politician who became chancellor of the exchequer in 1970, Iain Macleod, who coined the phrase in his speech to Parliament in 1965.
	In the version of Keynesian macroeconomic theory which was dominant between the end of WWII and the late-1970s, inflation and recession were regarded as mutually exclusive, the relationship between the two being described by the Phillips curve.
Employment	Employment is a relationship between two parties, usually based on a contract, one being the employer and the other being the employee.
Great Depression	The Great Depression was a severe worldwide economic depression in the decade preceding World War II. The timing of the Great Depression varied across nations, but in most countries it started in 1930 and lasted until the late 1930s or middle 1940s. It was the longest, deepest, and most widespread depression of the 20th century.
	In the 21st century, the Great Depression is commonly used as an example of how far the world's economy can decline.
Consumer	A consumer is a person or group of people, such as a household, who are the final users of products or services. The consumer's use is final in the sense that the product is usually not improved by the use.
Deflation	In economics, deflation is a decrease in the general price level of goods and services. Deflation occurs when the inflation rate falls below 0% (a negative inflation rate). This should not be confused with disinflation, a slow-down in the inflation rate (i.e., when inflation declines to lower levels).
Consumption	Consumption is a major concept in economics and is also studied by many other social sciences. Economists are particularly interested in the relationship between consumption and income, and therefore in economics the consumption function plays a major role.
	Different schools of economists define production and consumption differently.
Financial capital	Financial capital is money used by entrepreneurs and businesses to buy what they need to make their products or to provide their services to the sector of the economy upon which their operation is based, i.e. retail, corporate, investment banking, etc.
Recession	In economics, a recession is a business cycle contraction. It is a general slowdown in economic activity. Macroeconomic indicators such as GDP (gross domestic product), investment spending, capacity utilization, household income, business profits, and inflation fall, while bankruptcies and the unemployment rate rise.

19. Aggregate Supply and Aggregate Demand,

CHAPTER HIGHLIGHTS & NOTES: KEY TERMS, PEOPLE, PLACES, CONCEPTS

Capital	In economics, capital goods, real capital, or capital assets are already-produced durable goods or any non-financial asset that is used in production of goods or services. Capital goods are not significantly consumed in the production process though they may depreciate. How a capital good or is maintained or returned to its pre-production state varies with the type of capital involved.
Crisis	A crisis is any event that is, or is expected to lead to, an unstable and dangerous situation affecting an individual, group, community, or whole society. Crises are deemed to be negative changes in the security, economic, political, societal, or environmental affairs, especially when they occur abruptly, with little or no warning. More loosely, it is a term meaning 'a testing time' or an 'emergency event'.
Economy	An economy or economic system consists of the production, distribution or trade, and consumption of limited goods and services by different agents in a given geographical location. The economic agents can be individuals, businesses, organizations, or governments. Transactions occur when two parties agree to the value or price of the transacted good or service, commonly expressed in a certain currency.
Expenditure	In common usage, an expense or expenditure is an outflow of money to another person or group to pay for an item or service, or for a category of costs. For a tenant, rent is an expense. For students or parents, tuition is an expense.
Financial crisis	The term financial crisis is applied broadly to a variety of situations in which some financial assets suddenly lose a large part of their nominal value. In the 19th and early 20th centuries, many financial crises were associated with banking panics, and many recessions coincided with these panics. Other situations that are often called financial crises include stock market crashes and the bursting of other financial bubbles, currency crises, and sovereign defaults.

19. Aggregate Supply and Aggregate Demand,

CHAPTER QUIZ: KEY TERMS, PEOPLE, PLACES, CONCEPTS

1. In economics, _____ goods, real _____, or _____ assets are already-produced durable goods or any non-financial asset that is used in production of goods or services.

    _____ goods are not significantly consumed in the production process though they may depreciate. How a _____ good or is maintained or returned to its pre-production state varies with the type of _____ involved.

    a. Capital
    b. CAPRI model
    c. Cash crop
    d. Casa grande

2. _____ is the increase in the market value of the goods and services produced by an economy over time. It is conventionally measured as the percent rate of increase in real gross domestic product, or real GDP. Of more importance is the growth of the ratio of GDP to population (GDP per capita), which is also called per capita income. An increase in per capita income is referred to as intensive growth.

    a. Bad bank
    b. Bank failure
    c. Economic growth
    d. Bundism

3. The term _____ refers to economy-wide fluctuations in production, trade and economic activity in general over several months or years in an economy organized on free-enterprise principles.

    The _____ is the upward and downward movements of levels of GDP (gross domestic product) and refers to the period of expansions and contractions in the level of economic activities (business fluctuations) around its long-term growth trend.

    These fluctuations occur around a long-term growth trend, and typically involve shifts over time between periods of relatively rapid economic growth (an expansion or boom), and periods of relative stagnation or decline (a contraction or recession).

    a. Bad bank
    b. Business cycle
    c. Jewish Social Democratic Party
    d. Communist Bund

4. . In economics, _____ are the outcome of human efforts to meet the wants and needs of people. Economic output is divided into physical goods and intangible services. Goods are items that can be seen and touched, such as books, pens, salt, shoes, hats, and folders.

    a. Consumables
    b. Goods and services
    c. Port centric logistics

19. Aggregate Supply and Aggregate Demand,

CHAPTER QUIZ: KEY TERMS, PEOPLE, PLACES, CONCEPTS

5. In mathematics, a _____ is a ratio between two measurements with different units. If the unit or quantity in respect of which something is changing is not specified, usually the _____ is per unit time. However, a _____ of change can be specified per unit time, or per unit of length or mass or another quantity.

   a. Bank rate
   b. Bootstrapping
   c. Cash accumulation equation
   d. Rate

ANSWER KEY
19. Aggregate Supply and Aggregate Demand,

1. a
2. c
3. b
4. b
5. d

You can take the complete Online Interactive Chapter Practice Test

for 19. Aggregate Supply and Aggregate Demand,
on all key terms, persons, places, and concepts.

No Additional Costs

http://www.Cram101.com

Register, send an email request to Travis.Reese@Cram101.com to get your user Id and password.

Include your customer order number, and ISBN number from your studyguide Retailer.

20. Fiscal Policy and Monetary Policy,

CHAPTER OUTLINE: KEY TERMS, PEOPLE, PLACES, CONCEPTS

_____ Budget deficit _____

_____ Federal budget _____

_____ National debt _____

_____ Debt _____

_____ Hong _____

_____ Economic growth _____

_____ Government debt _____

_____ Demand _____

_____ Transfer payment _____

_____ Transfer payments multiplier _____

_____ Fiscal policy _____

_____ Multiplier _____

_____ Supply _____

_____ Automatic stabilizer _____

_____ Economic forecasting _____

_____ Forecasting _____

_____ Full employment _____

_____ Balance _____

_____ Rate _____

_____ Recession _____

_____ Monetary policy _____

20. Fiscal Policy and Monetary Policy,
CHAPTER OUTLINE: KEY TERMS, PEOPLE, PLACES, CONCEPTS

_____ Policy

_____ Federal funds

_____ Federal funds rate

_____ Aggregate demand

_____ Exchange rate

_____ Expenditure

_____ Interest rate

_____ Investment

_____ Real interest rate

_____ Inferior good

_____ Inflation

_____ Inflation targeting

_____ Bernanke

_____ Dual mandate

_____ Great Depression

_____ Money multiplier

_____ Money

20. Fiscal Policy and Monetary Policy,

CHAPTER HIGHLIGHTS & NOTES: KEY TERMS, PEOPLE, PLACES, CONCEPTS

Budget deficit	A government budget is a government document presenting the government's proposed revenues and spending for a financial year. The government budget balance, also alternatively referred to as general government balance, public budget balance, or public fiscal balance, is the overall difference between government revenues and spending. A positive balance is called a government budget surplus, and a negative balance is a government budget deficit.
Federal budget	In economics, a federal budget is a plan for the Federal government's revenues and spending for the coming year.
National debt	Government debt (also known as public debt and national debt) is the debt owed by a central government. (In the U.S. and other federal states, 'government debt' may also refer to the debt of a state or provincial government, municipal or local government). By contrast, the annual 'government deficit' refers to the difference between government receipts and spending in a single year, that is, the increase of debt over a particular year.
Debt	A debt is an obligation owed by one party (the debtor) to a second party, the creditor; usually this refers to assets granted by the creditor to the debtor, but the term can also be used metaphorically to cover moral obligations and other interactions not based on economic value. A debt is created when a creditor agrees to lend a sum of assets to a debtor. Debt is usually granted with expected repayment; in modern society, in most cases, this includes repayment of the original sum, plus interest.
Hong	The Hongs were major business houses in Canton, China and later Hong Kong with significant influence on patterns of consumerism, trade, manufacturing and other key areas of the economy. They were originally led by Howqua as head of the cohong.
Economic growth	Economic growth is the increase in the market value of the goods and services produced by an economy over time. It is conventionally measured as the percent rate of increase in real gross domestic product, or real GDP. Of more importance is the growth of the ratio of GDP to population (GDP per capita), which is also called per capita income. An increase in per capita income is referred to as intensive growth.
Government debt	Government debt is the debt owed by a central government. (In the U.S. and other federal states, 'government debt' may also refer to the debt of a state or provincial government, municipal or local government). By contrast, the annual 'government deficit' refers to the difference between government receipts and spending in a single year, that is, the increase of debt over a particular year.
Demand	In economics, demand for a good or service is an entire listing of the quantity of the good or service that a market would choose to buy, for every possible market price of the good or service.

20. Fiscal Policy and Monetary Policy,

CHAPTER HIGHLIGHTS & NOTES: KEY TERMS, PEOPLE, PLACES, CONCEPTS

	(Note: This distinguishes 'demand' from 'quantity demanded', where demand is a listing or graphing of quantity demanded at each possible price. In contrast to demand, quantity demanded is the exact quantity demanded at a certain price.
Transfer payment	In economics, a transfer payment is a redistribution of income in the market system. These payments are considered to be non-exhaustive because they do not directly absorb resources or create output. In other words, the transfer is made without any exchange of goods or services.
Transfer payments multiplier	The Transfer payments multiplier is the multiple by which Aggregate demand will increase, when there is an increase in transfer payments (e.g. welfare spending, unemployment payments). Changes in spending usually lead to a larger than one for one increase in Aggregate demand, because any increase in household incomes caused by the increase in spending also increases in consumption spending, which further increases Aggregate demand.
Fiscal policy	In economics and political science, fiscal policy is the use of government revenue collection and expenditure (spending) to influence the economy. The two main instruments of fiscal policy are changes in the level and composition of taxation and government spending in various sectors. These changes can affect the following macroeconomic variables in an economy:•Aggregate demand and the level of economic activity;•The distribution of income;•The pattern of resource allocation within the government sector and relative to the private sector. Fiscal policy refers to the use of the government budget to influence economic activity.
Multiplier	In economics, a multiplier is a factor of proportionality that measures how much an endogenous variable changes in response to a change in some exogenous variable. For example, suppose variable x changes by 1 unit, which causes another variable y to change by M units. Then the multiplier is M.
Supply	In economics, supply refers to the amount of a product that producers and firms are willing to sell at a given price all other factors being held constant. Usually, supply is plotted as a supply curve showing the relationship of price to the amount of product businesses are willing to sell.
Automatic stabilizer	In macroeconomics, automatic stabilizers describes how modern government budget policies, particularly income taxes and welfare spending, act to dampen fluctuations in real GDP. The size of the government budget deficit tends to increase when a country enters a recession, which tends to keep national income higher by maintaining aggregate demand. There may also be a multiplier effect. This effect happens automatically depending on GDP and household income, without any explicit policy action by the government, and acts to reduce the severity of recessions.
Economic forecasting	Economic forecasting is the process of making predictions about the economy.

20. Fiscal Policy and Monetary Policy,

CHAPTER HIGHLIGHTS & NOTES: KEY TERMS, PEOPLE, PLACES, CONCEPTS

	Forecasts can be carried out at a high level of aggregation--for example for GDP, inflation, unemployment or the fiscal deficit--or at a more disaggregated level, for specific sectors of the economy or even specific firms.
	Many institutions engage in forecasting, including international organisations such as the IMF, World Bank and the OECD, national governments and central banks, and private sector entities, be they think tanks, banks or others.
Forecasting	Forecasting is the process of making statements about events whose actual outcomes have not yet been observed. A commonplace example might be estimation of some variable of interest at some specified future date. Prediction is a similar, but more general term.
Full employment	Full employment, in macroeconomics, is the level of employment rates where there is no cyclical or deficient-demand unemployment. It is defined by the majority of mainstream economists as being an acceptable level of unemployment somewhere above 0%. The discrepancy from 0% arises due to non-cyclical types of unemployment.
Balance	In banking and accountancy, the outstanding balance is the amount of money owed that remains in a deposit account (or a loan account) at a given date, after all past remittances, payments and withdrawal have been accounted for. It can be positive (then, in the balance sheet of a firm, it is an asset) or negative (a liability).
Rate	In mathematics, a rate is a ratio between two measurements with different units. If the unit or quantity in respect of which something is changing is not specified, usually the rate is per unit time. However, a rate of change can be specified per unit time, or per unit of length or mass or another quantity.
Recession	In economics, a recession is a business cycle contraction. It is a general slowdown in economic activity. Macroeconomic indicators such as GDP (gross domestic product), investment spending, capacity utilization, household income, business profits, and inflation fall, while bankruptcies and the unemployment rate rise.
Monetary policy	Monetary policy is the process by which the monetary authority of a country controls the supply of money, often targeting a rate of interest for the purpose of promoting economic growth and stability. The official goals usually include relatively stable prices and low unemployment. Monetary economics provides insight into how to craft optimal monetary policy.
Policy	A policy is a principle or protocol to guide decisions and achieve rational outcomes. A policy is a statement of intent, and is implemented as a procedure or protocol. Policies are generally adopted by the Board of or senior governance body within an organization whereas procedures or protocols would be developed and adopted by senior executive officers.

20. Fiscal Policy and Monetary Policy,

CHAPTER HIGHLIGHTS & NOTES: KEY TERMS, PEOPLE, PLACES, CONCEPTS

Federal funds	In the United States, federal funds are overnight borrowings between banks and other entities to maintain their bank reserves at the Federal Reserve. Banks keep reserves at Federal Reserve Banks to meet their reserve requirements and to clear financial transactions. Transactions in the federal funds market enable depository institutions with reserve balances in excess of reserve requirements to lend reserves to institutions with reserve deficiencies.
Federal funds rate	In the United States, the federal funds rate is the interest rate at which depository institutions actively trade balances held at the Federal Reserve, called federal funds, with each other, usually overnight, on an uncollateralized basis. Institutions with surplus balances in their accounts lend those balances to institutions in need of larger balances. The federal funds rate is an important benchmark in financial markets.
Aggregate demand	In economics, aggregate behavior refers to relationships between economic aggregates such as national income, government expenditure and aggregate demand. For example, the consumption function is a relationship between aggregate demand for consumption and aggregate disposable income. Models of aggregate behavior may be derived from direct observation of the economy, or from models of individual behavior.
Exchange rate	European Monetary System was an arrangement established in 1979 under the Jenkins European Commission where most nations of the European Economic Community (EEC) linked their currencies to prevent large fluctuations relative to one another. After the demise of the Bretton Woods system in 1971, most of the EEC countries agreed in 1972 to maintain stable exchange rates by preventing exchange rate fluctuations of more than 2.25% (the European 'currency snake'). In March 1979, this system was replaced by the European Monetary System, and the European Currency Unit (ECU) was defined.
Expenditure	In common usage, an expense or expenditure is an outflow of money to another person or group to pay for an item or service, or for a category of costs. For a tenant, rent is an expense. For students or parents, tuition is an expense.
Interest rate	An interest rate is the rate at which interest is paid by a borrower for the use of money that they borrow from a lender (creditor). Specifically, the interest rate is a percent of principal (P) paid a certain amount of times (m) per period (usually quoted per annum). For example, a small company borrows capital from a bank to buy new assets for its business, and in return the lender receives interest at a predetermined interest rate for deferring the use of funds and instead lending it to the borrower.
Investment	Investment is time, energy, or matter spent in the hope of future benefits. Investment has different meanings in economics and finance.

20. Fiscal Policy and Monetary Policy,

CHAPTER HIGHLIGHTS & NOTES: KEY TERMS, PEOPLE, PLACES, CONCEPTS

Real interest rate	The real interest rate is the rate of interest an investor expects to receive after allowing for inflation. It can be described more formally by the Fisher equation, which states that the real interest rate is approximately the nominal interest rate minus the inflation rate. If, for example, an investor were able to lock in a 5% interest rate for the coming year and anticipated a 2% rise in prices, they would expect to earn a real interest rate of 3%.
Inferior good	In economics, an inferior good is a good that decreases in demand when consumer income rises, unlike normal goods, for which the opposite is observed. Normal goods are those for which consumers' demand increases when their income increases. This would be the opposite of a superior good, one that is often associated with wealth and the wealthy, whereas an inferior good is often associated with lower socio-economic groups.
Inflation	In economics, inflation is a sustained increase in the general price level of goods and services in an economy over a period of time. When the general price level rises, each unit of currency buys fewer goods and services. Consequently, inflation reflects a reduction in the purchasing power per unit of money - a loss of real value in the medium of exchange and unit of account within the economy.
Inflation targeting	Inflation targeting is an economic policy in which a central bank estimates and makes public a projected, or 'target', inflation rate and then attempts to steer actual inflation towards the target through the use of interest rate changes and other monetary tools. Because interest rates and the inflation rate tend to be directly related, the likely moves of the central bank to raise or lower interest rates become more transparent under the policy of inflation targeting. Examples:•if inflation appears to be above the target, the bank is likely to raise interest rates.
Bernanke	Ben Shalom Bernanke is an American economist at the Brookings Institution who served two terms as chairman of the Federal Reserve, the central bank of the United States from 2006 to 2014. During his tenure as chairman, Bernanke oversaw the Federal Reserve's response to the late-2000s financial crisis. Before becoming Federal Reserve chairman, Bernanke was a tenured professor at Princeton University and chaired the department of economics there from 1996 to September 2002, when he went on public service leave. From 2002 until 2005, he was a member of the Board of Governors of the Federal Reserve System, proposed the Bernanke Doctrine, and first discussed 'the Great Moderation' -- the theory that traditional business cycles have declined in volatility in recent decades through structural changes that have occurred in the international economy, particularly increases in the economic stability of developing nations, diminishing the influence of macroeconomic (monetary and fiscal) policy.

20. Fiscal Policy and Monetary Policy,

CHAPTER HIGHLIGHTS & NOTES: KEY TERMS, PEOPLE, PLACES, CONCEPTS

Dual mandate	A dual mandate is the practice in which elected officials serve in more than one elected or other public position simultaneously. This practice is known as double jobbing in Britain and distinguished from double dipping in the United States, which refers to being employed by and collecting retirement from the same public authority at the same time. For example, a candidate is elected mayor of a town or wins a seat on a local authority at an election, then the same person wins a seat in the national or state/provincial legislature in a separate general election, this is a dual mandate.
Great Depression	The Great Depression was a severe worldwide economic depression in the decade preceding World War II. The timing of the Great Depression varied across nations, but in most countries it started in 1930 and lasted until the late 1930s or middle 1940s. It was the longest, deepest, and most widespread depression of the 20th century. In the 21st century, the Great Depression is commonly used as an example of how far the world's economy can decline.
Money multiplier	In monetary economics, a money multiplier is one of various closely related ratios of commercial bank money to central bank money under a fractional-reserve banking system. Most often, it measures the maximum amount of commercial bank money that can be created by a given unit of central bank money. That is, in a fractional-reserve banking system, the total amount of loans that commercial banks are allowed to extend (the commercial bank money that they can legally create) is a multiple of reserves; this multiple is the reciprocal of the reserve ratio, and it is an economic multiplier.
Money	Monetary disequilibrium theory is basically a product of the Monetarist school mainly represented in the works of Leland Yeager and Austrian macroeconomics. The basic concept of monetary equilibrium (disequilibrium) was, however, defined in terms of an individual's demand for cash balance by Mises (1912) in his Theory of Money and Credit. Monetary Disequilibrium is one of three theories of macroeconomic fluctuations which accord an important role to money, the others being the Austrian theory of the business cycle and one based on rational expectations.

20. Fiscal Policy and Monetary Policy,

CHAPTER QUIZ: KEY TERMS, PEOPLE, PLACES, CONCEPTS

1. In economics, a _____ is a redistribution of income in the market system. These payments are considered to be non-exhaustive because they do not directly absorb resources or create output. In other words, the transfer is made without any exchange of goods or services.

   a. Family cap
   b. Transfer payment
   c. Mixed economy
   d. Poverty pimp

2. _____ is the debt owed by a central government. (In the U.S. and other federal states, '_____' may also refer to the debt of a state or provincial government, municipal or local government). By contrast, the annual 'government deficit' refers to the difference between government receipts and spending in a single year, that is, the increase of debt over a particular year.

   a. Bad bank
   b. Government debt
   c. Local currency
   d. Prime Risk

3. In economics, a _____ is a plan for the Federal government's revenues and spending for the coming year.

   a. Black budget
   b. Civil list
   c. Confidence and supply
   d. Federal budget

4. European Monetary System was an arrangement established in 1979 under the Jenkins European Commission where most nations of the European Economic Community (EEC) linked their currencies to prevent large fluctuations relative to one another.

   After the demise of the Bretton Woods system in 1971, most of the EEC countries agreed in 1972 to maintain stable _____s by preventing _____ fluctuations of more than 2.25% (the European 'currency snake'). In March 1979, this system was replaced by the European Monetary System, and the European Currency Unit (ECU) was defined.

   a. Exchange rate
   b. Development aid
   c. Bond
   d. Commerce raiding

5. . In economics, a _____ is a business cycle contraction. It is a general slowdown in economic activity. Macroeconomic indicators such as GDP (gross domestic product), investment spending, capacity utilization, household income, business profits, and inflation fall, while bankruptcies and the unemployment rate rise.

   a. Recession
   b. Constant maturity credit default swap

20. Fiscal Policy and Monetary Policy,
CHAPTER QUIZ: KEY TERMS, PEOPLE, PLACES, CONCEPTS

c. Credit default swap
d. Cuyahoga Land Bank

ANSWER KEY
20. Fiscal Policy and Monetary Policy,

1. b
2. b
3. d
4. a
5. a

You can take the complete Online Interactive Chapter Practice Test

for 20. Fiscal Policy and Monetary Policy,
on all key terms, persons, places, and concepts.

No Additional Costs

http://www.Cram101.com

Register, send an email request to Travis.Reese@Cram101.com to get your user Id and password.

Include your customer order number, and ISBN number from your studyguide Retailer.

Other Facts101 e-Books and Tests

Want More?
JustTheFacts101.com...

Jtf101.com provides the outlines and highlights of your textbooks, just like this e-StudyGuide, but also gives you the PRACTICE TESTS, and other exclusive study tools for all of your textbooks.

Learn More. *Just click*
http://www.JustTheFacts101.com/

CPSIA information can be obtained
at www.ICGtesting.com
Printed in the USA
BVOW09s0232060217
475395BV00004B/111/P